The
Complete
Hogan

A Shot-by-Shot Analysis
of Golf's Greatest Swing

JIM McLEAN
with
TOM McCARTHY

WILEY

John Wiley & Sons, Inc.

Copyright © 2012 by Jim McLean. All rights reserved

Photo on page 9 by Alex J. Morrison

Published by John Wiley & Sons, Inc., Hoboken, New Jersey
Published simultaneously in Canada

For general information about our other products and services, please contact our Customer Care Department within the United States at (800) 762-2974, outside the United States at (317) 572-3993 or fax (317) 572-4002.

Wiley also publishes its books in a variety of electronic formats and by print-on-demand. Some content that appears in standard print versions of this book may not be available in other formats. For more information about Wiley products, visit us at www.wiley.com.

Library of Congress CataLoging-in-Publication Data:
McLean, Jim, date.
 The complete Hogan : a shot-by-shot analysis of golf's greatest swing
Jim McLean and Tom McCarthy.
  p. cm.
  ISBN 978-0-470-87624-4 (cloth : alk. paper); ISBN 978-1-118-11621-0 (ebk);
ISBN 978-1-118-11622-7 (ebk); ISBN 978-1-118-11623-4 (ebk)
 1. Swing (Golf) 2. Hogan, Ben, 1912–1997. I. McCarthy, Tom, 1949– II. Title.
 GV979.S9M3 2012
 796.352'3—dc23

                                                                2011042285

Printed in the United States of America

10 9 8 7 6 5 4 3 2 1

Contents

Foreword

by Ken Venturi

Jimmy McLean has been my friend since we first met back in 1976. Jimmy got to know my great friend Franny Santangelo, and it was Franny who put the two of us together that summer at Westchester Country Club in Rye, New York. Later that winter Jim came out to Palm Springs where I continued my work with him on his golf game.

When I taught any professional, I often did it "on the golf course." We were usually playing at Bermuda Dunes. So Jim McLean and I played a lot of golf together. In 1977 he missed at the final stage of PGA tour school and came to work for me when I ran the Marco Island Club in Florida. One great thing about Marco Island was that my old friend Gene Sarazen lived there. So Jim played with Gene many times, along with the rounds of golf and teaching I continued to do with Jimmy.

During the summers Jim returned to New York as a teacher at Westchester Country Club, then later became the head professional at three of the top clubs in New York. When he moved up the ladder to a new head professional position, I would always go see him and play. Since I was doing my analyst work for CBS, I would be in New York for the tour event, and inevitably Jim would be working with several tour professionals. He would always have me come over to give some ideas.

The thing I know about Jim McLean is his deep interest in the workings of the golf swing. At the top of his list is Ben Hogan, who was a close friend of mine. Jim never tired of hearing about that relationship or anything I ever learned or noticed about Hogan. I was blessed to work with and play with the two greatest ball strikers and players maybe of all time, Byron Nelson and Ben Hogan. I passed a lot of that knowledge along to Jim, and he has passed it along to many other tour players.

That is a legacy of Hogan. Everyone wanted to know his secret. Guys like Gene Sarazen, Gardner Dickinson, Jackie Burke, and me know there were many qualities that made Hogan great. Surely his golf swing was one, but there was also a whole lot more.

I'm proud I knew Hogan well and feel very blessed that I could watch and learn from him. I first played with him in my first Masters in 1954, second round. Thereafter, except in 1955 when I was overseas in the military, we played the back nine every Wednesday afternoon before the first round of the Masters.

This book provides phenomenal images of Hogan in 1947 and 1948 when he was at the height of his talent, before the accident. Nobody took down a golf course like Hogan. I saw that in the 1950s. Like Hogan, I had my career cut short right in the prime of my golf life. Jim points this fact out beautifully inside these pages.

You're going to learn more than you could ever expect. Jimmy McLean learned from great players how to teach. I was happy to share my best thoughts on the golf swing with him. Nobody I have ever known has shown as much interest in and dedication to teaching the game of golf. This guy leaves no stone unturned. He teaches ideas that have stood the test of time, not one-shot-wonder methods.

Ben Hogan worked a lifetime to perfect his swing. No book has shown you how he did it. This one does.

Watching Hogan

I have been a huge Ben Hogan fan since I first saw him play in the fall of 1968 at Champions Golf Club in Houston. Rick Belden, my teammate on the University of Houston golf team, was a member there, and he would call me whenever Hogan showed up. I'd arrive before Rick could put down the phone. Together we watched Hogan play seven or eight informal rounds, and were the only ones shadowing his group.

I also watched Hogan practice on the range at Champions, and I examined his every move. The greatest athletes in any sport have a certain aura. You can see it in the way they move and how those around them give them their full attention. That's one thing I would certainly say about Hogan: he captured your full attention, and it was hard not to watch his every move.

Hogan went to the far side of the Champions range on the days I watched him hit balls. He always had a shagger, a caddy who put the shag bag right in front of his feet. When I watched those shots I observed that each one fell slightly right and that the shagger almost never moved. Every shot zeroed in on that shag bag like a laser. The caddy would, at the most, make a small step left or right to snag the shot, never more.

Rick wrote the following in an e-mail after he learned I was writing this book: "Isn't it amazing that we were able to watch Ben Hogan so closely with almost nobody around. The shot shape. The ball always falling to the right . . . no left for Hogan, it didn't exist. Even with a varying wind condition the man was like a machine."

I agree with Rick and only wish I had somehow filmed those rounds of golf we watched. The thing about Hogan was that if you saw him on a golf course, you never forgot it. That picture always stays with you, the sound of his shots sizzling through the air and the unbelievable control. Everyone who ever watched him knew it was different and knew it was special.

His playing companions, in time, would become as special to me. They were Jackie Burke and Jimmy Demaret, the owners of Champions, and Jackie's brother Jimmy, the club's head pro. All of them played hundreds of rounds of golf with Hogan and were true friends of his, and I'm proud to say they are also friends of mine. They knew Hogan both on and off the golf course. All grew up in Fort Worth, Texas. Jimmy was Hogan's lifetime friend. I didn't know Jackie's father, but I sure heard a lot about him. Demaret called Jack Burke Sr. his second father. I bring up Jack Burke Sr. because he mentored Demaret, and later Hogan would make his secret adjustments by copying Demaret's grip and ball flight, the power fade.

If watching Hogan play provided an introductory survey to his craft, they offered the graduate degree, and it was long in coming. From them I gained several lifetimes' worth of observations about how he played the game, things that could never be gleaned from film study.

I was also very fortunate to spend a good deal of time with the legendary Sam Snead. He was, of course, a contemporary of Hogan's during the 1946 to 1948 years. Sam and I did a comprehensive videotape together in 1999. I spent three days at the Homestead in West Virginia with Sam, and also did two special Golf Channel shows on him. I went to the Masters with Sam twice and stayed in the same house with him. Although Sam and Hogan were competitors, Sam had a deep respect for Hogan. He always had great things to tell me about him, except for one thing that always bothered him. That was 1950, when Sam won ten PGA events while Hogan won only one. However, that one was the U.S. Open, and one must assume as a result that Hogan received Player of the Year from the PGA of America. Sam said he was stunned when that happened and never really got over it.

I loved my long talks and my work with Gary Player as much as he loved watching Hogan, especially the athleticism in Hogan's swing. Gary did not miss a thing on Hogan. He was built the same way and had the same will and desire to be great. Both won nine majors. Gary told me the secret to great ball striking was "a total release of the club, but with no fear of a hook." Hogan could do this.

At the Commemorative, a Senior Tour event, I had numerous conversations about Hogan with the great Lee Trevino, who said he too copied Hogan. Few people would ever suspect that. No, he didn't copy his swing exactly. Rather, he copied the ball flight, Hogan's controlled fade. To do it Lee had to aim as far left as possible, then hit as far right as possible. It was an ingenious idea on his part. He eliminated the left side of the golf course, like Hogan.

In addition, I've studied the writings of Bobby Jones and feel very comfortable saying that Hogan used many of the same descriptions and phrases written previously by Jones. I know Hogan admired everything about Jones, not the least of which was his intellect, and, of course, his advice and teachings on the golf swing. Even masters have masters.

In my desire to learn everything I could to understand Hogan's swing, I've even done something I probably shouldn't have. I was a member of the University of Houston golf team (we won the NCAA championship two times and finished second the other two years I was there), and I had access to the golf shop and the bag room at Champions, so I was able to sneak in and pick up Hogan's clubs. I took most of them out of the bag and swung his driver. I'm not sure what you know about his golf clubs, but they had oversized cord grips. We had heard that Hogan used a coat hanger to form the rib, a slightly raised section running up and down the length of the grip that is also referred to as a reminder, and as I gripped those clubs I certainly felt it. What hands Hogan had! Those clubs were heavy, the rib set weak (meaning to the left of the grip's center) to accommodate the grip change he made in 1945 and 1946. Picking up those clubs after watching him play was something I will never forget. (You know Hogan played with no glove.) I'm just glad he didn't walk in!

I mention all this to demonstrate that what you'll read in this book comes from him, from his friends, and from my direct observations of him, as well as my decades of film study. If there's opinion, it's informed opinion. Too often those who write about Hogan see him from the grandstand, not from the tee. That will not be the case here.

This book looks at Hogan's swing more closely than anything ever done, my aim to describe clearly and concisely its key components. The book will give you the opportunity, via its rare photographs, to look at and observe Hogan yourself. So it offers you a chance to experience Hogan in a manner that's only second best to having watched him play or hit balls yourself. And along the way I will show you how you can integrate Hogan's mechanics into your own game.

The key to this book, what would make it like no other, was to get film of Hogan at his very best and then use sequential stills from it to show the details and the important motions of his entire golf swing. A single drawn illustration or photograph of Hogan is usually totally worthless in identifying the secrets to his swing. But in this book you will be able study his perfect blend of clubhead, clubshaft, hands, ankles, knees, hips, shoulders, and head motion. Hogan's swing was like a symphony of movements, with an ideal sequential development of power, and by viewing it closely you will have an ideal model for your own swing. For this reason I've included the frame numbers for each still from the respective films so you can get a sense of the rhythm of Hogan's swing and the beats it hits.

For these pictures and, indeed, for the idea of this book, I have Tom McCarthy to thank. Over many years at Doral I watched him accumulate a huge Hogan collection. He collects everything having to do with golf instruction—photos, books, and films—but mostly film and photos about Hogan through four decades, the 1930s through the 1960s. This material would be the basis for the three-part DVD series I helped Tom develop, *The Ben Hogan Collection*.

From this library I have chosen the best photographs from the late 1940s. The prevailing thinking of most golfers and instructors is that Hogan was better after the terrible 1949 car accident that severely injured him. Specifically, they point to

1953, when he won three major championships. But Hogan himself told Jim Kelly in a television interview that he played his best golf in 1947 and 1948, and this book will prove him correct.

The perfect face-on angle series, filmed at Riviera Country Club in 1948, is first in the book and is its centerpiece. I've never seen a more perfect view of Hogan anywhere. The second sequence, showing Hogan down the line, came from film shot in 1947. And the third series of photographs is from the 1948 Masters from a forty-five-degree angle, one of my favorite views to study. Each image includes a lengthy discussion about its place in the logical progression of the swing, with many offering advice you might apply to your own game.

I will cover important topics such as the grip, the waggle, the two-plane swing, the left hip action, lateral motion, rotation and turning movements, head position, cupping the left wrist, rotating the left arm, supination or the bowing of the left wrist at impact, the long right arm, and a straight, balanced finish. In addition, I will discuss Hogan's use of big grips and stiff shafts, and how from his swing we learned how the big muscles guide the swing, the hips, and the legs, leading the shoulders in the downswing while the arms are connected to the body, eliminating any conscious hand action or manipulation.

So that you can best appreciate these series, I will first walk you through the development of Hogan's swing and its elements and many secrets, several heretofore unheralded. Afterward I'll offer you Hogan's own drills. I only wish to make the book so complete that I could include that sound of his club hitting the ball, the warmth of a perfect Houston day, and the excitement of a young man watching a legend.

1

The Many Secrets of Hogan's Swing

Ben Hogan began developing his legendary golf swing early in his career. He quickly adopted Harry Vardon's overlapping grip, which was a very strong grip with the left hand easily showing three or four knuckles on the top of the clubshaft. In 1937 Harry Cooper (known on the PGA Tour as "Pipeline" for how straight he hit the ball) had a serious instruction session with Hogan where he told Hogan that his grip loosened at the top. Harry told me that Hogan corrected the problem, then used this idea of maintaining a solid position at the top for the rest of his life. Later, in 1939, with the help of Henry Picard, Hogan weakened his strong grip to a more neutral position to take a bite out of the big hook he was playing in tournaments and long-drive competitions and that too often put him in trouble. These two sessions alone propelled Hogan to the top of the game, making him the leading money winner in 1940, 1941, and 1942.

In the 1930s Hogan had the opportunity to watch and learn from the legendary teacher Johnny Revolta, particularly on his use of a "waggle" in preparing to hit a shot. What impressed Hogan was Revolta's use of the waggle as a precursor and mini simulation of the coming golf shot. The waggle established the clubhead's path on the backswing and an overall swing rhythm or tempo. Revolta (who was also a PGA champion) told me that he showed Hogan how to change the waggle according to the varying golf shots required in different circumstances. This was a big revelation for Hogan, one for which Revolta is not given enough credit.

Revolta may have also taught Hogan what many think of now as the Hogan finish. Theirs are the same as Hogan's, with the left shoulder far around, the left upper arm parallel to the ground, and the clubshaft bisecting the head, but it was Revolta who taught that finish.

Throughout his early career Hogan experimented extensively to improve his golf swing. Ideas came from other players and top teachers of the time. He used trial and error and would select a key swing feature, then test it, retest it, discard it if it did not hold up to tournament play, or incorporate it on a permanent basis if it did by hitting many balls in practice. Hogan was very intuitive and used the empirical evidence of how swing changes held up under tournament pressure, not just on the range. Obviously, many of the sound golf body mechanics taught today were originally proven correct by Hogan through his experimentation on the range and execution on the golf course.

When Hogan was discharged from active duty after World War II he charged into the tournament golf circuit and won at a pace that stunned both his fellow competitors and the golf world. In late 1945 and early 1946 he was playing great golf and posted wins and top ten finishes that earned him terrific prize money for that time. He was still unsatisfied with his golf swing, however, because he lacked the level of confidence in it that he both wanted and knew he needed to reach his great potential. The dogged appearance of the inaccurate hook during tournament rounds continued to hurt his overall score and finish position in tournaments and therefore, of course, his earnings. This inconsistency ground him down, and he finally took a "sabbatical" from the rigors and distractions of the tournament schedule in order to analyze his golf swing at home in private. All the years of study and practice allowed him to bring his legendary focus to the analysis of his problem, the occasional surprise hook.

Finally, his solitary analytical method yielded an answer. He would proclaim it as a eureka moment, which he said came to him as an idea after he woke up one morning. Hogan had found the final swing "secret," later announced by his brother Royal to golf writers. Hogan tested this new method privately on the range, and then secretly out on tour. In 1955, after much speculation by everyone concerned with the game and after his golf career was starting to wind down, Hogan offered up his secret to *Life* magazine. The disclosure included a weakened grip with the left hand turned an eighth of an inch counter-clockwise along with a slight V cupping of his left wrist at the top of his backswing, which opened the clubface more than it had been previously.

I'm certain he actually copied the exact Demaret grip. Jackie Burke told me he was certain the last grip change came from Hogan's observations watching Jimmy Demaret hit his beautiful consistent fade. For Hogan, the grip change and this cupping of his wrist and concurrent opening of the clubface yielded a consistent power fade that had wonderful trajectory, distance, accuracy, and, most important, consistency under pressure. He could now absolutely count on the fade as well as work the ball any way he wanted.

With his newly acquired arsenal of refined swing technique, elevated confidence, and determination, Hogan marched back out on tour in 1946 and began establishing one of the best tournament winning stretches in golf history.

Or so the story goes.

Most observers are sure there are more than just the two secrets Hogan revealed in *Life*, and quite a few teachers, writers, and players have tried to identify the "real" Hogan secret. Nobody, though, has done it to the satisfaction of the public. Most of the claims have been wild guesses made with hardly any research. The rest have been done on very shaky examination, often from still pictures from all kinds of angles. Many other observations involve trying to determine what he did that was so unique. Again, these have been made from looking at photographs taken at random camera angles or possibly video from different odd angles, which renders this sort of research worthless. You cannot compare the action in videos or photographs shot from different angles.

To do comparative research you must shoot video from precise angles and from the proper height. Carl Welty and I have been doing this for forty years, and our method of filming is the same used by Trackman, the launch monitors used by the PGA Tour. These and all other launch monitors are set straight down the target line. Carl figured this out fifty years ago when he had the CEO of Hughes Missile Systems, Bill Glasson, who was also very involved with NASA and America's first space launch, build him his first clubhead and swing path computer back in the 1960s. Carl had filmed down the line when he first used a camera at PGA Tour sites back in the late 1950s. Using the new Swing Speed machine only confirmed his thinking on down-the-line filming. Most important, it gave us a simple way to film a player the same way every time. You place the camera on the intended target line at a specific height and far enough away from the player to avoid distortion.

When you film a player face on, again you must be precise. For example, I can make your swing look more upright by placing the camera high, or flatter by placing it low. If I set up my camera forward of the body, then the ball placement will look farther back in the stance.

You can see just how important this is for conducting an accurate study. Most golf instructors, however, pay little attention to the details of filming, and many if not most golf artists and golf writers have no idea about comparative golf research, so how could any of them possibly give detailed and accurate information? The photos you get from general shots are again completely random, and again are useless for accurate research. The video shot by most people is all over the place, and the camera they use is often handheld (not on a tripod). You cannot be "almost correct" with video or film. It has to be precise.

The down-the-line shots and the face-on shots of Ben Hogan in this book conform to what all of my teachers do, and what Carl taught me.

Perfect camera angles and decades of serious research have allowed me to make some very accurate comparisons and statements. That is how I came up with the information under each photo in this book—combined, of course, with the knowledge imparted to me (over many years) from Hogan's best friends and those who helped him progress with his swing.

I must also point out that Hogan developed all of his secrets well before the accident. It was a progression of important steps. The swing after 1949, after the accident, was phenomenal, too, but it was the swing Hogan resurrected, not the foundational one he built from scratch. So there was nothing fundamentally new there. The swing was still great and the mind was still incredibly strong, but it was not a new swing. It was built precisely on all of the ideas Hogan had discovered before the accident.

So here are the fifteen true secrets Hogan used to build the greatest game in the history of golf.

1. **Build major strength in the body and in the correct places.** At five foot seven, Hogan had exceptionally long, powerful arms and super-strong hands. He was in great shape from hitting thousands of golf balls and from labor ing when he was a boy. His legs were solid and his ankles very flexible. He was quick. Some of this is obviously God-given, but anyone can do an excellent job in building a sound body. Remember too that Hogan entered the army and went through basic training. He continued military training for two and a half years. Hogan's military basic training also consisted of a series of exercises that anyone could do, such as push-ups, towel squeezes, sit-ups, and light weights. Surely hitting thousands of golf balls builds up your golf muscles. Hogan steeled his body but did not build up the chest or shoulders. He maintained great flexibility.

2. **Tension relief.** Hogan copied the great Johnny Revolta's waggle. It was a huge revelation to him, and he mastered his own version of a preliminary waggle that served several functions: relaxing his wrist joints, elbows, and shoulders just prior to the swing (as well as providing other benefits mentioned elsewhere in this book). He melded these preliminary moves with his refined body movements. Together the waggle and his pre-swing movements produced a preparatory flow that took away tension prior to making his swing. Hogan adjusted the waggle for the various types of shots he would play. It prepared him

physically and mentally for the shot at hand, thereby again reducing tension. You can clearly see the preparatory movements in the photos.

I've never heard anyone describe the Hogan waggle correctly and never read about it anywhere either. It is not correctly illustrated in *Five Lessons*, but I will help you learn more about it here. Hogan actually moved his left arm toward the target in his waggle as you can see in the photographs. He waggled twice, not once. He waggled the club up above the ball toward the target, back over the ball, and into a mini backswing, dramatically opening the clubface. Also, it has never been noted before, but Hogan took his left elbow off his left side. The left arm was bent, not straight, very relaxed. This is a very different description of Hogan's waggle from the one he gave in *Five Lessons*, and there were not enough illustrations in that book to show this feature. Nobody but Carl Welty has ever figured this out, and he deserves all of the credit.

3. **Into position in three moves.** First, Hogan always set up to the ball in the same way. This allowed him to place the ball precisely where it needed to be in his stance for each and every shot. He always stepped in with his right foot first while placing the clubhead behind the ball. Ken Venturi explained Hogan's pre-shot procedures to me many times, and of course I watched Ken do it every time himself when we played.

    Step in with the right foot, placing the clubhead down directly behind the ball. Hogan always set the left foot before dropping the right foot into position next. By placing the left foot first he could get the ball exactly where it needed to be in relation to the left heel.

Third, he set the right foot into its address position, and this established the width of the stance he wanted for each particular shot. Hogan changed his stance for the variables he faced on the course, such as shots played into the wind, downhill shots, draw shots, sidehill shots, short irons, driving, and so on. The secret was his ability to ingrain the three steps with a precise routine. Set the club down first, then the left foot, and then the right foot. In these three simple moves Hogan blended the setup into his waggle. He developed this routine during the late 1930s when Harry Cooper worked on his setup and helped him adjust his grip of the club. I think it was actually a combination of Revolta, Henry Picard, and Cooper that influenced Hogan's setup procedure the most.

4. **Vivid belief in the shot image.** Before Hogan hit any shot he narrowed his focus. He burned an intense, vivid image into his mind of the trajectory, spin, and landing spot of his shot. Ken told me that Hogan felt this "belief" that you could hit the shot required was the most important key to success, more important than any swing mechanics. If a player could vividly picture and then execute his swing with total confidence, the chances of pulling off the shot were extremely high, even if that person's swing mechanics were not great. That's how powerful the mind was, according to Hogan.

5. **Groove the takeaway.** Hogan wrote extensively on the takeaway, but his instruction on this first part of the swing has been far underestimated. Again, Ken hammered this home to me in my lessons with him and in our many rounds of golf together.

How this could go so unnoticed is a mystery to me. It is something I always teach my students and is a big part of my golf school training. With practice, anyone can pick up this move for their own game.

Hogan said the takeaway is a recoil from the forward press. The first move in the backswing is actually a slight move toward the target, then the club rebounds away. By studying the face-on view of Hogan in this book you can clearly see it. Hogan called it one of the two crossroads in the swing, and he meant that the takeaway set up the entire backswing motion. What I mean here is that the backswing must start away all together, with the hands, arms, shoulders, and club. It's called a "one-piece takeaway." I watched Ken work with great players like Tom Watson, Tom Weiskopf, John Cook, Ben Crenshaw, and many others on the move away from the ball. He always wanted me to remember the importance of the Hogan concept of taking the club away in a one-piece groove.

I thought it was very interesting that George Knudson always sat down on a bag and watched Ken hit balls. He was a huge Hogan fan and asked Ken many questions about Hogan. George, a Canadian, is considered one of the all-time great ball strikers who employed the Hogan one-piece takeaway.

Remember, the key to a one-piece takeaway is in getting all of the major movements synchronized as you begin the swing, and the beauty of it is that it can be repeated under pressure. Hogan learned to "slot" his takeaway every time. This was a secret move he developed during the early 1940s, as he became the PGA Tour's leading money winner. You will observe this takeaway vividly in the photos.

6. **The 1946 adjustments.** Hogan has written in detail about the two small adjustments he made in 1946 to open the clubface slightly more in his backswing. However, the real secret of the two adjustments was not exactly revealed. Hogan weakened his left-hand grip by moving the left thumb an eighth of an inch to the left and more on top of the club. The second adjustment was in opening the club-face during the backswing by rotating the left forearm and putting a very small cup in the left wrist at the top of the backswing. The real secret evolved from these two adjust-ments. The key was that the *clubface stayed open* as Hogan started the downswing. With the cup in the wrist and the clubface laid open, Hogan could release everything as hard as he could. From the open position he could bow the left wrist and just keep the left arm pinned to his body through impact. That's why the swing became "hook proof," and why Hogan was able to achieve his longtime goal of totally eliminating the hook.

"Hogan hated a hook," Claude Harmon told me at lunch one day in Rancho Mirage, California. "Ben would rather have a coral snake slithering around his body under his shirt than hit one hook, and you know the coral snake is the most poisonous snake in the world."

7. **The two-way move.** Ken Venturi showed me Hogan's "fall onto the left side" move, something Claude Harmon also observed, taught, and talked to me about. Both Ken and Claude won majors, and both worked with many top tour players, which should be recommendation enough for anybody.

The move is difficult for most of us to do—in fact, I made some mistakes myself early in my playing career by not making this move the right way—because there is no top of the backswing. While the club was still going back, Hogan leaned his body forward and onto a stacked left side. However, there's a big misconception with some modern instruction that Hogan stacked his left side on the backswing. This is absolutely incorrect. Hogan stacked the left side with the two-way move. First he stacked the right side in the backswing. Don't miss this crucial move as you study Hogan's swing. It is very athletic move, and it looks awesome when done correctly. When Hogan got onto his left leg he could then turn his left hip as fast as possible. This is what he wrote about and demonstrated. However, his demonstration left out the lean to the left.

Again, look at the photos. Hogan makes a major shift forward (toward the target), while the clubhead is clearly going backward. This "fall move" keeps the club back as long as possible with the body always leaning forward. It gives the feel of the left arm pulling, but it is really the left side and the big muscles of the body doing so. There is no conscious pulling of the left arm and no effort required to produce a tremendous amount of club lag, meaning that the club is trailing behind the leaning and pivoting motion of the body. Yet make no mistake about it: the club is trailing the body, and as Hogan always stated, this meant that he could never hit "over the top." To me this two-way move is perhaps Hogan's biggest secret of all.

The move will not be easy to incorporate into your game, so I've taken pains to point it out in my discussion of the pictures. And you will have to take pains to practice it.

8. **The bow.** An obvious secret used by Hogan, discernible to all who observed closely, was the counterclockwise action of the left forearm and the left wrist coming into impact.

The man who stressed this idea the most to me personally was Claude Harmon, who called it hitting "into the bow." By that he meant that the back of the left wrist had an outward bow at impact, with, as Hogan himself wrote in *Five Lessons*, the wristbone both raised and heading the action forward. He referred to this left wrist action through impact as "supination," meaning that the left palm is down through impact. Hogan stressed that this added both speed to the clubhead, because it facilitated clubhead rotation, and distance to the shots, because the action delofted the clubface slightly. The poor player, Hogan explained, makes the exact opposite movement with his left hand through impact, meaning he pronates it (the left wrist breaks down—dorsid flexion), and in so doing disrupts the arc of the swing and adds loft to the club, which results in a loss of distance on the shot.

Hogan shows this left wrist action very clearly in his first book, *Power Golf*, and Anthony Ravielli does a fantastic drawing of the bow in the second book, *Five Lessons*. Hogan wanted no breakdown of the left wrist. Claude said that Hogan's left wrist was like Bethlehem steel. Many teachers picked up on those illustrations, and the idea of hitting with a flat or bowed wrist is a staple of modern instruction. They do usually miss the position of the left arm where the left arm is fixed in space through impact and the inside of the left elbow is pointed outward. Observe the sequence of Hogan photos through impact to see this for yourself.

An important change that Hogan made in his swing strongly coincides with his bowing of the left wrist, and that is the grip adjustment he made in 1946. By weakening the left hand—again, meaning that he turned it to the left on the club's grip, while repositioning his slightly shorter thumb more on top, rather than to the right side of the grip—Hogan could bow the wrist with no fear of hitting a hook. If you have a strong grip and try to bow the wrist you will close the clubface at impact and hit lots of low hooks, the very shots Hogan set out to eliminate from his game. So the grip change was also a key to bowing the wrist. His left thumb points down at the ball during impact, something I described in the *Power Line* DVD.

9. **The long right arm.** Hogan made one of the greatest moves into the ball ever seen in the game of golf. His lower body was so powerful and coordinated that it looked like he was about to run down the fairway. It was explosive, forceful, and committed. Another secret move taught to me by Ken Venturi was Hogan's long right arm after he made contact with the ball. At impact the right arm still had bend, but post-impact it straightened, and it stayed straight far into the finish. Hogan wrote about the long right arm in *Power Golf*, but Ken gave me an idea I have used often in my teaching. He said that Hogan gave the impression that he was hitting four balls. By that Ken meant that the club appeared to "stay on the ball" a longer time. Hogan's extension of his right arm through the impact zone is something to be studied and copied.

The secret move I'm talking about here also involved the right hand. Hogan's right hand worked slightly under after impact, meaning it did not display a full-roll release over the left hand. You can see this when you look at Hogan's halfway-through/post-impact position in this book. At that point in his swing his left wrist cups and his right wrist goes flat, or even bowed. That is a big secret of the long right arm. Almost nobody has ever described the Hogan postrelease correctly. The full extension of the right arm long into the follow-through, combined with a non-turned-over right wrist resulted in tremendous distance with tremendous control.

10. **The straight, balanced finish.** Although Hogan absolutely hit into a bowed left side, which you can vividly see in the photos by noting the bend in both his knees and torso, the continuation of his right side (right shoulder, right hip, and right arm) got him to a straight, stand-up finish. Part of the finish was the position of the golf club, particularly the clubface. If you look closely you will see that the toe of the club is down and the clubface is pointing away from the target. This has everything to do with the Hogan hand action and is largely unnoticed as a secret. I have to credit Gardner Dickinson for showing me this Hogan gem.

If you practice this finish you will get the feel of how Hogan's hands worked differently from most golfers through the post-impact section of the swing. A key element of this difference is simply that Hogan continued and sustained his post-impact motion for a longer time and through a larger arc than almost anyone else. That's why the toe of his club pointed down and the face of the club away from the target. So it is the total of the Hogan finish that is the secret nobody talks about.

Hogan hit more golf balls than almost anyone, yet suffered no back problems even after the accident (he did suffer mightily from the other injuries). Therefore, he could practice as much as he wanted. In modern golf it seems that many tour players develop bad backs, as of course do many amateurs. Since hard practice, covered in the next secret, was crucial to Hogan's success, you must look at how he kept his body in such fantastic golf condition. Many modern teachers try to have their students "stay in their posture long into the follow through," which will cause back injuries. I look to Hogan's follow-through and see a player at ease and comfortable. Remember, when you copy Hogan's finish, as so many great players have, you must also look to the unnoticed secret of the shaft position, the hand position, and the clubface. The left wrist is broken inward, knuckles facing away from the target, and the shaft is nearly horizontal. The most copied finish in golf is not usually copied accurately.

11. **Practice habits.** After his practice sessions, Hogan wrote detailed notes on what he was practicing and why he was practicing it. He wrote down how it worked on the range and then out on the course in competition. As Jackie Burke said, "Some changes did not make it from the range to the first tee with Hogan." He also always practiced by hitting shots to a shagger, a person positioned down the practice fairway to retrieve the balls, and this automatically narrowed his focus. Hogan greatly preferred to practice into the wind or in a right-to-left wind. He would not practice much with a left-to-right wind or downwind, in part because he felt such a wind threw him off balance while he swung.

When he worked on his fade he would always go to the far right side of the range, so that he had the entire width of the practice range to start his ball left then fade it back to the right. This way, Ken Venturi said, his eye "saw the fade" better. Hogan looked for practice situations that "fit his eye," an idea all golfers could benefit from using. Claude Harmon told me that Hogan would go to a certain place at Seminole Golf Club to practice the fade, next to the 16th hole where the wind was coming off the Atlantic Ocean from the right. He said Hogan might practice slicing shots for three hours at a time, all morning. Then they would have lunch and tee off at 1 p.m., and Hogan would hit blistering fades, with just a dash of left to right, but never any hooks. He would practice at Seminole for months during the winter, preparing for the Masters and the remainder of the golf season. Claude said Hogan would hit it dead perfect on the golf course day in and day out and that his practice sessions always included at least some severe slice shots.

The rest of Hogan's secrets deal with the mental and management parts of the game. Yet these secrets had a major positive influence on his swing confidence and his shotmaking ability.

12. **A photographic memory.** Both Johnny Bulla and Gardner Dickinson spoke about Hogan's considerable mental and intellectual gifts as a major secret of his ability to hit great shots, and it's a secret that is also too often overlooked. All of Hogan's friends knew the power of his memory, his ability to organize and recall the shots he had hit from various points on golf courses from years gone by. He had the ability to remember everything about a course he had already played. This is incredibly important when reading greens. It's a skill Tiger Woods has talked about as one of his gifts. Tiger has said he can remember the exact breaks from the greens he played five years ago. Hogan could do the same. These two great golfers shared the gift of total recall. What an advantage and what a great secret.

13. **Putting on the blinders.** Hogan perfected the ability to shut out all outside interference. This is a skill today's

sports psychologists try to teach modern players. Hogan invented the total zone focus for golf. There are many stories regarding his focus, including the famous story from the Masters when Hogan played with Claude Harmon. Claude made an ace on the 12th hole, and Hogan did not even know it. All he ever said on the course, according to Jimmy Demaret, was, "You're away." Hogan said that he could create in his mind huge walls down the side of each fairway that could not be penetrated by stray shots. A friend of mine made the comment that Hogan "looked like he was playing alone." Ask yourself, when have you played your best golf? I'll bet playing alone some evening. Well, Hogan played as if he were alone even in the majors! He barely knew who his playing partners were, and it really did not matter to him. He played the golf course. His concentration was second to none. Think about his nicknames and they reveal this secret: "the Iceman" and "the Hawk." These were perfect descriptions of the man, even though his incredible mental prowess remains perhaps not fully recognized as one of his true secrets.

14. **Body language.** Hogan wore only the finest, custom-tailored clothing. Tommy Bolt and Doug Sanders, both very cutting-edge dressers, commented to me that nobody looked better in clothes than Hogan. He had movie-star looks and highlighted that with the best of the best outerwear. He began creating this image as soon as he could afford to, beginning in the late 1930s. Everything about his appearance was as sharp as could be. When he showed up at any tournament he was the best-dressed man there. Many people have commented on Hogan's appearance. What they have not said is that this was one of his secrets. His look and the body mannerisms he employed were

absolutely meant to intimidate the opposition. He walked like an athlete. He walked with confidence, and he was in perfect condition. If anyone ever walked like a champion, it was Hogan. You never saw Hogan mope, whine, or make excuses. He was a winner who exuded a positive aura at all times and a definite feeling of being above the fray.

John Wooden, arguably the greatest basketball coach ever, gave me a card that I still keep in my wallet. It says, "Don't whine. Don't complain. Don't make excuses." Champions live by these maxims.

15. **Total preparation.** Hogan deciphered each thing in his life and made sure it was done correctly. He made everything manageable by thorough preparation. He left little or nothing to chance. "Total preparation" was another of his big secrets.

To be prepared on a golf course and to be able to play smart golf, Hogan developed one shot he could depend on no matter what the circumstance: the fade. Ken Venturi said that if you put a gun to Hogan's head and told him he had to hit the fairway, he could do it. This fade was his slam-dunk shot, which he knew he could call upon every time, under any condition, and under any amount of pressure.

It is one thing to develop a plan of attack for a tournament golf course, but it is entirely different to execute the plan. Hogan could do both. The point here is the requirement and the importance of having a "go-to" shot. In an interview I did with Ben Crenshaw about Hogan, he said, "Ben Hogan was like a general planning the perfect military operation as he set up his game plan for a major championship. Hogan planned better than anyone in the history of the game, and then he was able to execute the shots necessary to follow the plan." Nobody ever prepared better. Like Sun Tzu wrote in *The Art of War*, "Every battle is won before it is fought."

These fifteen secrets represent the fundamentals I gleaned from my own study of Hogan and his game and from thoughts I've developed in discussion with Hogan's friends and confidants. Combined, they form the key elements that made Hogan so special, although of course there were many other things that made him a great player. It was a compilation of the fifteen major secrets working in conjunction with all of the other smaller elements of his game and personality that produced the swing and game that will forever live in the annals of golf.

Jackie Burke, Hogan's great friend, always bristled when somebody said Hogan had five fundamentals. Jackie knew that was crazy. He knew Hogan made small adjustments throughout his career.

The key thought here, and one that you will find important to remember, is that golf is a game of adjustments and improvements. All great players adjust throughout a year or career. The great ones, however, have a strong foundation built upon sound principles. When they fall into a bad patch of golf they have fundamentals to fall back upon. Unlike many golfers, they don't look for a new swing, or some new method of swinging. They have a trust and belief in their own set of fundamentals. Most golfers have no real "center." In this analysis of Hogan I have given you the elements of his true center and the fundamentals he always went back to.

Once Hogan came up with his secrets to playing great golf, he did not deviate from them. Gardner Dickinson told me that Hogan always went back to his core keys, and they were only a few. Lots of golfers have hundreds of things they will try.

Hogan never did that. The fifteen secrets I outlined may seem like a lot, but in golf you could easily find fifteen hundred ideas to work on. I'm a big believer in "being brilliant at the basics." That saying is on the walls of all of my schools, and it comes from working with the greatest golf minds ever developed in America, who are mentioned and quoted throughout this book. It's my pleasure to share them with you.

Hogan built his game piece by piece. There was no sudden leap to greatness. He just kept improving. That is the intriguing part of his mystique. He figured the game out, and he left many clues to how he did so.

Through the years I've done a comprehensive study of Hogan's swing and listened to all of the theories put forth about it. I've read all of the Hogan books, even ones that are written by complete amateurs that contain only brief conversations with pro golfers. I feel confident that I know not only his true secrets, but also how he executed them, including methods that have never previously been revealed. I've also alluded to the "little things" that contributed to his success, such as that he did not wear a glove and that he used extra-stiff shafts in his clubs. Did these elements really help him? Emphatically, yes they did!

The secrets Hogan developed were all accomplished by 1946. From that time forward he had mastered the keys to his phenomenal ball striking. The machine was built. That's what this book sets straight. From that time forward Hogan had the swing and the game that will no doubt be studied for as long as golf is played. It is a swing that has never been matched.

2

The Three Sides
of a Swing

There are several other elements of Hogan's swing that while they are not included in the fifteen fundamentals, are worth describing at length before we get into our film study.

The Backswing

Hogan started the backswing with a small recoil off the left side and by slightly turning his chin away from the target. Like Jack Nicklaus and Tiger Woods, Hogan was left-eye dominant. If you are right-eye dominant, like most right-handers, this

Hogan head turn will not work well. You will lose sight of the ball.

Something almost nobody I have ever talked to mentions, and nothing I have read refers to, is the front of Hogan's book *Five Lessons*, which contains a fantastic drawing of the body as a machine. The engine of this machine was in its core, the center of gravity. Hogan believed in the linking of movements, the transmitting of power through a chain of movements. This linkage would create an exponential increase in power in the golf swing. Hogan wrote about the multiplying effect of the chain action, with the hips leading the way.

Hogan described the swing plane in his famous image of a pane of glass sitting on top of the shoulders and extending down to the ball. It is the most frequently used visual in teaching golf. When I teach I draw a line from the center of the ball to the top of the shoulders just as Hogan showed in *Five Lessons*. In continued honor of Hogan I have called this the Hogan Plane in my lessons and teachings and in my best-known book, *The Eight-Step Swing*.

Hogan wrote that the shoulders would turn on this plane line. The left arm would stay under the pane of glass or ideally brush against it at the top of the backswing. If the left arm is under the pane of glass at the top of the backswing then the odds are that it would be parallel to the pane. Hogan said it was not disastrous if the left arm was on a slightly flatter plane, but it should never rise or lift above the pane of glass, "shattering" it. This proper position of the left arm in relation to the plane and the left shoulder was very critical as Hogan changed direction to start the downswing. Nobody, up to this point in golf, had so clearly explained these different planes.

The Downswing

Hogan said the downswing plane was less steeply inclined than the backswing plane. In other words, the shaft fell to a shallower plane and thus the downswing plane constituted a second plane. He also wanted the plane to aim slightly more to the right (inside out), with its bottom edge slightly elevated, which is largely a visual illusion. With correct use of the body, the club falls onto this second plane with no conscious effort. In teaching many average golfers I might have to physically move the clubshaft with them in order to get that feel. The pane of glass in effect shifts and orients out to the right (for a right-handed golfer). Hogan was clear on how and why this happened correctly. The pane of glass shifts as a result of the leg and hip action in the downswing and guarantees an inside attack track into impact.

Brilliantly, Hogan changed his plane and angle of attack for the different clubs in his bag. For example, he played a short iron with an open stance, which, combined with a more upright angle, gave his shots a blow downward and left (great ball strikers make divots with their irons that point slightly leftward). Tour players now know that these simple adjustments make shots with the lofted clubs go straight.

Conversely, Hogan played his driver with a closed stance, which, combined with the ball forward in his stance and a lower downswing plane, gave him a very shallow angle of attack and thus an ascending blow with the driver.

Although Hogan wrote about immediately turning his hips to the left (an Anthony Ravielli illustration shows this with a large rubber band attached to Hogan's left hip), he actually wrote that "there must be enough lateral motion forward to transfer the weight to the left foot." For some inexplicable reason, most people who read or discuss (or take the drawing literally) Hogan's *Five Lessons* miss this crucial point. Turning the hips without the lateral move is a major mistake. "As long as you made *enough lateral motion*," Hogan wrote, "you cannot move the hips too fast." In fact, he further wrote, "the faster the better." But first you have to get onto that left leg. That's key. I explain the "fall" onto the left leg in the face-on sequence photos of Hogan's swing in chapter 4.

Ravielli also drew the arms from the face-on view at setup incorrectly; it was not at all what Hogan actually looked like. Also, the drawing of Hogan's turn was not like the real deal. Ravielli's drawings of Hogan looking down the line were much better.

Hogan was adamant that golfers of every level, beginners to advanced players, limit the use of the hands. He wanted no conscious manipulation with the hands. The hands and wrists do not roll. In *Five Lessons*, Hogan details this action.

As mentioned previously, a popular method first introduced in 2008 called "Stack and Tilt" advocated a reverse weight shift on the backswing, and used Hogan as an example of a great player who turned on his left leg in the backswing. Andy Plummer and Mike Bennett, the creators of Stack and Tilt, use still photographs to prove their point, but this shows how pictures can fool you.

Here's the big problem: the photos they use to try "to prove the reverse pivot point" are "still shots" taken after Hogan has already started forward. They are also taken from all kinds of different angles. This is just a small example of inaccurate conclusions taken from analyzing still photos. I have used only perfect face-on angles from a film sequence to show you what Ben Hogan really did. His head moves to the right. He does shift weight. There is no reverse pivot. Hogan stacked the right side first, adding width and power, before making the lateral move onto a stacked left side. That's a huge difference from the Stack and Tilt's prescribed golf swing.

Many teachers say that Hogan wished he had "three right hands," but Hogan also wrote that you hit the ball as hard as you can with both hands: "You must hit as hard with the left as with the right." What's more, Hogan wrote in *Five Lessons* that he wished he had three right hands in terms of applying power to the ball, not "to hit with," as it is commonly misquoted. In other words, Hogan felt the power his swing had generated channeling through his hands and into the club; he never taught to flip the right hand at the ball, bending the wrist forward. Never!

In the downswing, Hogan wrote that the right elbow leads the arm as you start down. I use this idea with many amateurs who tend to throw the club from the top. It's a great part of his book to study.

Another true fundamental that appeared in Hogan's writings is that the downswing arc is inside or more narrow than the backswing arc. This is another overlooked fundamental that stands the test of time. I have thought this fundamental as so important that I actually use a version of it for my Jim McLean Golf Schools logo. I also include it as one of my "22 Fundamentals of Top Ball Strikers" (from *The Eight-Step Swing*, third edition).

When you observe the photos in this book, you will see that at impact Hogan's right elbow is still slightly bent. It is not until two feet past the ball that the right arm fully straightens out, resulting in maximum acceleration of the clubhead through the point of impact with the golf ball. Hogan wrote that once the right arm straightens it stays straight to the finish of the swing. It's what Ken Venturi called the "long right arm"—another Hogan idea that will be taught forever. Ken worked with many tour players on the wide extension of the right arm, and it was fun to watch him demonstrate the move in person. This long right arm is another Hogan idea that Tiger Woods has copied. Tiger makes practice swings that look identical to Hogan's. I've watched him do it many times at Doral, Augusta, and the U.S. Open.

Ken always favored a more flat lie angle on his irons. All of his clubs were bent flat like Hogan's. The iron shots I watched Ken hit for a long expanse of time were awesome. Ken told me Hogan expected him to hit the correct shot to various pin locations: Low draw to the back pin. High fade to the front location. Low fade, three-bounce iron shot to the back right pin. That's the kind of stuff I saw Ken do all of the time. We played together for a decade and nobody hit better iron shots than Ken. Absolutely awesome. When I compared his swing to Hogan's you could see what Ken incorporated from the man. Ken would always say that Hogan was the greatest ball striker he ever saw. When you think that Ken was the lead analyst at CBS for thirty-four years and won sixteen PGA Tour events, plus a U.S. Open, you know he saw all the greats up to the writing of this book. Ken was among the best of them, and he learned a ton from playing and talking with Hogan.

Both Claude Harmon and Lee Trevino had a closed clubface at the top, unlike Hogan, but when you lay the clubshaft flatter during the downswing, you'll notice that the clubface automatically lays back and is more open. This is what Trevino did, which is why he didn't strike the ball with a closed clubface. This move also gets the right elbow in down and leading so that the clubhead is delivered inside the line and on the more shallow attack angle. A golfer, by having the left wrist bowed at the top of the swing (like Trevino), gains one advantage, in that he already has in place that same bowed left wrist he wants at impact. Hogan wanted and produced the bow at impact, though as I've said, he actually added a slightly cupped wrist at the top when he made the swing changes that would lead him on to true greatness. Trevino kept that bow in his left wrist all the way from the top through impact, whereas Hogan achieved the bowed left wrist at impact via the strong leftward rotation of his left forearm during the downswing and the supination (turning the palm upward) of his left hand and wrist through impact. These were two different methods to achieve the same impact condition of a bowed left wrist. The key, however, is the move starting down, which when done correctly, as, of course, both Hogan and Trevino did it, flattens the plane. In Trevino's case, this start downplane flattening move also squared up his clubface.

Current players with a closed or bowed left wrist at the top include the PGA Tour's leading money winner in 2010, Matt Kuchar; the tour's seven-time straightest driver, Fred Funk; and super-long young star Dustin Johnson, to name a few.

When Hogan's hands reached hip level on the downswing his belt buckle was already facing the ball. At impact the left leg is bowing out toward the target. Many players have a straight left leg at impact, and I wonder if this has contributed to the numerous left knee and lower back injuries experienced by golfers who follow this practice.

"Don't be afraid of swinging too hard," Hogan instructed, as he knew speed was a key fundamental for top ball strikers. "I can hit the ball straighter if I hit it hard and full," he said. I see this, for sure, on the PGA Tour. The top pros smoke the driver. Again, don't underestimate this tip.

Owning His Swing

I tell my students, "One of the hardest accomplishments in golf is to relax and just swing the club." Tiger Woods, in fact, said in a television interview in 2004 that he wanted a swing he "owned for major championships" and that achieving one was a big reason he changed teachers during this time. The changes he made ultimately did not lead to owning his swing, but his quest continues, as do all of ours. Hogan, though, owned his as of 1946.

In my experience and in talking to a wide array of professionals, I think you could say that Trevino and Hogan owned their golf swings at a level above all others. Like a great rifle shooter, they just did not miss. They had a swing that stamped out identical shots, trajectory, and distance control at an unimaginable level. At just a fraction below you had Sam Snead, Jack Nicklaus, Byron Nelson, Nick Price, and Bruce Lietzke.

Other great players have had more wide-open games and could scramble like magicians. I would include Arnold Palmer, Seve Ballesteros, Tom Watson, Phil Mickelson, and Tiger in this category. All of them could hit perfect golf shots. All could stripe it. Yet each of these players might hit a drive off the planet. Each of them had incredible power and major-league top-end speed.

A good way to check who is at the top of the ball striking list might be as follows: If you asked every person on the PGA Tour if they would trade their long game for Ben Hogan's, would any of them say no? I don't know that answer for sure, but it might be that all of them would make the trade.

Here's how I look at Hogan's golf swing in terms of owning it. Before the accident he was in total control of his game and had announced to the world that he had the secret. After the accident he could never again play week to week. Never again would he be "full-time tour player" or in the "tournament mode." Normally a player needs to play at least some kind of tournament schedule, or make some week-after-week planning for professional competition. Hogan never did after the accident.

Instead he played a very sporadic schedule. For example, Hogan played only four events in 1951 and won three. He played only three events in 1952 and won one. Then in 1953 he won all three majors while playing only in six PGA Tour events that year; he also won two others, making it five wins in six starts. And so it went until 1968, when he greatly reduced his competitive playing appearances.

As late as 1967, at the age of fifty-five, he finished tenth at the Masters. That was his first event of the year. The hills at Augusta National made it an exceptionally tough course for him to walk with his severe circulation problems. Yet he shot a flawless 67 in Saturday's third round. He would play three more events, including the U.S. Open, where he made the cut. Again, in 1967 he remarkably finished third at the Houston Championship and also third at Colonial.

Hogan again played three events in 1970, where I watched his practice rounds: at Champions Golf Club in Houston he finished in ninth place, at Colonial he finished T56, and finally the Westchester Classic in Rye, New York, where he was forced to withdraw.

I also saw Hogan at his last tour event in 1971 at Champions, where he wrenched his knee at no. 4 and withdrew at no. 10, unable to finish.

Even in 1970 and 1971 at Champions the other players stopped to watch Hogan on the range, and many of the tour players actually went out to watch him play. That never happens. Tour players do not run out to watch anybody play. Never. They did for Hogan.

And they sometimes needed to be put in their place. Let me share an interesting story very few people have heard about Hogan at that 1970 Champions event, which he entered as a huge favor to Jackie Burke and Jimmy Demaret. At that point in Hogan's life it was very rare for him to appear anywhere outside of his home course at Shady Oaks in Fort Worth. Thousands of people were sure to come watch him. Hogan asked Jackie Burke if he could practice over on Jack Rabbit, the club's second course, across the street from the more famous Cypress. On the 14th hole he could hit balls under ideal conditions and with nobody to bother him. The Gulf wind was normally into and slightly right-to-left most days, and the hole fit Hogan's eye for the preferred shot shape, his famous left-to-right fade into the countering wind. Jackie said absolutely. So that's how it went, Hogan hitting balls on the other course while rest of the tour players practiced on the Cypress range.

After the first round of play, one of the tour players came into the clubhouse and knocked on the office door where both Jackie and Jimmy Demaret resided. Jackie acknowledged the player and invited him in. This unnamed tour player immediately commented to Jackie, "I see that Ben Hogan is practicing over on the other course." Jackie responded, "That is correct." The player, expecting a better answer, said, "Well, that's not really fair. All the rest of us have to practice at the range here." Burke again said, "Correct." Then the player came up with the line Jackie was hoping for: he said, "Can I practice over there?" Jackie shot back a simple "No." The pro, as expected, asked, "Why not?" Jackie Burke said, "The very second you win sixty-three PGA Tour events and nine majors then I will put you right over there next to him with your own special shagger."

The thing is, Hogan was still delivering. His ball striking and swing were still there, even at his relatively advanced age and with his super-limited playing schedule.

When I produced the VHS tape (later a DVD) titled *Ben Hogan: The Golf Swing*, I went to Fort Worth to do some additional research. One of the neat things I did was play Colonial with Richard Speed as my caddy. Richard caddied for Ben Hogan there and also shagged golf balls for him whenever he practiced.

I had a fabulous day with Richard, who was sixty-eight years old when he caddied for me. He told me he was then an 8 handicap. We laughed all day and talked about his Hogan experiences.

Richard told me that Hogan shot 65, 66, 67 every time at Colonial. That was just average. Sometimes he shot lower. He always played for money if he was playing in a group. Once in a while he played alone. I asked Richard about the Hogan shot pattern. Richard said Hogan hit bullets, usually with a very slight fade. They looked almost dead straight. I asked Richard how Hogan played the famous "Horse Shoe" at Colonial (holes 3, 4, and 5). This is a brutal stretch of holes that are long, tight, and super tough. Richard said it was like watching a machine. He could not ever remember Hogan making a bogey. Richard also told me that in Hogan's later years he still could have shot in the low 60s if he putted like he used to as a younger man. He had lost almost nothing from his ball striking. When Richard shagged balls he swore to me that he rarely had to move. Hogan literally knocked down the shag bag from every distance.

Richard said Hogan was very serious but had a sense of humor and treated him very well.

Coming up the 18th hole that day, I saved my best question for last. I asked Richard that if he had to bet everything he owned, who would he bet on in a head-to-head match between Hogan and Tiger Woods? I was actually a little surprised when he immediately said Hogan. After all, Tiger was burning up the tour and had recently won the U.S. Open by 15 shots at Pebble Beach. I asked Richard why he chose Hogan. He replied, "Because Mr. Hogan did not miss shots, while Tiger will occasionally hit a shot off line. Mr. Hogan never did. He owned his swing."

When will we see another machine like this?

3

The Eight-Step Analysis

To me there are two distinct ways to strike a golf ball in a highly effective manner: the hands and arms concept best described by Ernest Jones, and the "big muscle swing" best described by Ben Hogan. In my book *The Eight-Step Swing*, I detail the differences. In this book I've stuck to all of the Hogan principles, ideas, and drills that I learned from my research, but it's helpful to use the eight-step swing as a way of tracking elements of Hogan's.

Using images from the face-on sequence, the following are the key checkpoints in Ben Hogan's swing that you can easily recall and imitate. They are the building blocks of your game.

Step 0

Step 0. Address

Hogan is balanced perfectly and has gone through his detailed pre-shot routine. His upper triangle (the two arms and shoulder line) of his setup is relaxed and directly over the lower triangle. The lower triangle would be his legs slanted equally inward, with the connecting line between the feet. The upper triangle sits directly over the lower triangle.

Step 1

Step 1. The Takeaway

Hogan called this very initial start-up move one of the two crossroads in the golf swing. It has to be done right. Basically it is simply a one-piece takeaway. From a solid setup position, the club is taken away from a very slight forward press of the body (a slight bump toward the target). There is then a smooth takeaway, which includes a very small shift to the right (away from the target). Hogan begins to load the right side early. It's done mostly with the shoulders and arms; however, although it is difficult to see, some weight has begun to shift, or load, into his right side, leg, and foot. With the clubhead approximately three feet off the ball the hands have done nothing except maintain a soft grip pressure on the club, which is very important.

Step 2

Step 2. Halfway Back

This is what I simply call the halfway-back position. It is a key checkpoint for everyone. You should look at Hogan's arms and clubshaft. The right arm is above the left. The shaft is parallel to the ground. The right side of Hogan's body is beginning to stack up. The weight is definitely onto his right side and has come off of his left side. There has been a slight drift of his body behind the ball. Remember that Hogan made less body movement with short irons than he did with his long irons, fairway woods, and driver, and he also set the club earlier with short irons than he did with the other clubs. This is a very important point.

Step 3

Step 3. Three-Quarter Backswing Completion

Notice that the angle between his left arm and the shaft has created the letter L. Hogan made no conscious effort to set the club, so this means his wrist joints remained flexible and relaxed. In other words, he created a 90-degree angle at Step 3 because momentum and a free swing action set the club automatically. At Step 3 Hogan looks very powerful, and it is right about here where he begins his transition move back to the ball.

Step 4

Step 4. Top of the Backswing

As noted, Hogan truly did not have a top of the backswing. There was no stop at the top and then a reverse move back down to the ball. Hogan was always in motion, meaning that relatively soon after the club began going back, his body had already started forward. This is simply a great athletic move that is used in throwing and hitting procedures by all the greats in all sports. Hogan and all great ball strikers do it essentially the same way. By the time we stop Hogan at the top, he has actually begun the "forward fall," as I term it. He is transferring weight back onto a forward-leaning left side. Yet his club is still traveling back. As a result, the load on the clubshaft increases dramatically. This great Hogan move creates somewhat of an illusion. The look of Hogan's super lag of the golf club trailing his hands, wrists, and arms is often misunderstood. It looks like he is intentionally increasing his wrist cock when in fact it is his body pulling on the shaft that establishes it. The hands are, again, passive, which, again, is an important key in creating that great amount of lag during his famous downswing.

Step 5

Step 5. Move Down to the Ball

I usually look at the transition at two points: Early Step 5, which takes place just as a golfer changes direction with his lower body first, and Late Step 5. Late Step 5 is halfway down and is an easy checkpoint and the one I'll focus on here. It's virtually a matchup with Step 2 in that the clubshaft is now halfway down and again parallel to the ground. It is a position I termed the "delivery position" way back in the early 1980s. Carl Welty and I were doing serious research and found that this halfway-down position predicted nearly everything that would happen at impact. Hogan called the transition move leading into Late Step 5 the second crossroad in the swing. I totally agree. How else can you explain the fact that every PGA, LPGA, European, Asian, South African, and Japanese tour player has a different backswing position at the top? None is the same. However, at Late Step 5 we see very much the same thing in all truly accomplished players. It's a key move and a vital position (shaft parallel to the ground) for you to practice and master.

Step 6

Step 6. Impact

Teachers call impact the moment of truth, because this is when you strike the ball. This is when and where your alignments have to be correct. It's so obvious that it's hard to disagree with these statements. However, there are many secrets to arriving at the moment of truth properly. For sure, impact does not resemble the setup position. This has long been a major misconception of the average golfer. You need to study Ben Hogan at Step 6, just prior to impact, carefully. Nobody has ever looked better. A few tips: notice the bowed left wrist, the left arm forward, the hips turned left, the right shoulder under and forward, head behind the ball, weight far forward, and the push off the right instep.

Step 7

Step 7. Post-Impact Extension and Early Follow-Through

In our golf schools we teach the "extension position" every day. Take a good look at the body positioning of Ben Hogan at the halfway-through position. Again at Step 7, I look at several locations, as I do in Step 5. The picture shown here is the key face-on position. Practice placing yourself in a similar position. Both of Hogan's arms are straight and fully extended, with the head beginning to release to the target.

Step 8. Swing Finish and Rebound

Nobody ever went to a more perfect finish than Ben Hogan. In chapter 1, I detailed all of the things I've learned in my research. It's a very long list. However, this picture shows most of what any player really needs. Hogan finishes in a straight and balanced posture. The clubshaft finishes aligned across the neck, and his head and eyes are up and looking directly down the target line, tracking the flight of the ball. I would recommend copying this finish. Do it over and over with practice swings until it becomes a habit. Then take it to the range and then finally to the golf course. It will do wonders for your game.

4

Face-On View

I start my detailed description of Ben Hogan's swing with a perfect face-on view. The year is 1948, and Hogan is hitting a 3-wood from the tee in front of a crowd of admiring spectators. The suits, hats, and other attire of the crowd provide a relative time indicator for this sequence, because we can use them as points of reference for Hogan's swing as it progresses from frame to frame.

You could fairly call this "The Best Ever View of Ben Hogan's Best Golf Swing," because it was filmed during his prime with a perfect face-on angle with the camera set on a tripod. No wonder there have been and still are so many great tour players who say Hogan's swing was the best golf swing of all time. Learn by closely studying what he did in this swing. Hogan further improved his swing via the diligent research he conducted, and of course an unmatched practice ethic, and it brought him phenomenal success. The swing was ultimately validated by the distance and accuracy he consistently achieved on a day-to-day basis, year after year, and even after a devastating accident. Remember, it is also the swing (and the year) that Hogan himself proclaimed his game as "the best it ever was."

I'll now dissect the King of Swing from three key angles. The first is a thirty-nine-frame face-on sequence.

Frame 000

Addressing the Ball, Hogan's Pre-Swing Preparations

The Hogan waggle. Although Hogan described his waggle several times in clinics, it was not really described precisely in *Five Lessons*, and as a result few have copied it correctly. Study this picture. The left elbow is bent and forward of the body. The left hand is forward. The right wrist is fully cocked. The clubface is open. The clubhead is way off the ground. The body is quiet. If you study the drawings in *Five Lessons* you will get this position wrong, because it is drawn incorrectly with the left arm on the body. This picture is the real deal. I want to point out how physically soft Mr. Hogan appears in his movements throughout this first set of photos. By soft, I mean that there is no evidence of tightness in any part of his body as he goes through the preparatory movements for his swing. One can discern no tension in the legs and none in his arms or shoulders. He is freely swinging the club back in what is called the waggle, letting the action of fully cocking his wrists push his right arm and hand, as well as the left along with it, toward the target as his right wrist is bent fully back.

My first professional teacher, Al Mengert (who worked for both Claude Harmon and Tommy Armour), told me a great story on this subject. His wife, Donna, took film of Al at a U.S. Open. She had extra film left so she also filmed Ben Hogan. When the film came back about two weeks later Al eagerly watched his swing. He completely forgot Hogan was on the film. After Al's swings ended, unexpectedly the Hogan swing popped up. Al commented immediately that he looked like a robot, while Hogan looked like Fred Astaire, the great dancer. What a tremendous description of Hogan's setup and swing. Smooth as silk. You can see in the photo at least a 90-degree angle between his right hand and his right forearm at the extreme position of the waggle. His left arm and elbow are forward, toward the target, past his left hip and pants pocket. Not at all like the drawings in *Five Lessons*. But what does this mean? I think it means that Hogan executed his true waggle in a much more free-flowing and full manner than the *Five Lessons* drawings communicate.

Hogan has already taken his stance in this photograph and aligned his feet parallel or slightly closed to the target line, with his right foot flared several degrees out and not at a right angle to the target line as he would write in *Five Lessons*. From Hogan's point of view the right foot might appear to be at close to a 90-degree angle. Yet this motion picture analysis and the photos derived from it show precisely where the feet are placed. The right toe is flared just slightly (but perhaps looked squared off from his view as a player), which helped him to brace the right leg in the backswing and then to push off in the downswing. The left foot would appear to Hogan to be a quarter turn out toward the target. Hogan was correct in this description in his book.

Hogan always used the left foot to spot or locate his ball position in relation to his stance for every shot. In the countless hours I spent with Ken Venturi he would express how beautifully Hogan set up to every shot. It had burned a vivid image in Ken's mind. I never forgot it and have taught it ever since.

Hogan has tilted his hips forward so that his right leg develops an angle most evident at the knee. His left leg is also angled inward. Jackie Burke said, "The lower body also forms a triangle." The first triangle is formed by the arms and shoulders. One can see, as Jackie says, that the second triangle is formed by the legs and hips.

All of these pre-shot movements and positions prepared Hogan to generate a tremendous swing speed through the impact zone. Hogan swung the golf club as if it were a whip, not a sledgehammer. In fact, I think his swing could be fairly described as a crack of the whip. He was able to achieve this by keeping his body and hands relaxed, swinging along the proper plane, and using his legs and hips to bring his arms and the golf club through the hitting area. Hogan's idea of peak club-head speed was beyond the ball, not at the ball, but it is important to remember that this was his feel and the mental image and goal he had in his mind while he swung. He of course knew that the club's impact with the ball slowed the speed of the swing down, so its fastest point in fact happened before impact, not after it. Again, the important point is that he strove to achieve maximum acceleration through the ball strike. This acceleration might account for the unique sound that spectators heard when Hogan hit the golf ball. It has been said that Hogan hit balls as if they were fired from a cannon. The sound was that distinctive.

FACE-ON VIEW
. . . .

Nobody has ever described the modern "big muscle swing" better than Ben Hogan. My friend Jimmy Ballard used many examples of Hogan when he became the most famous teacher of his era (in America). Jimmy also taught in the Swedish Golf Federation for many years. Annika Sorenstam's swing perfectly exemplified what Ballard taught, though she may not have worked directly with him on her swing. However, whether she knows it or not, Ballard via Hogan had a huge impact on her golf swing and on those of many of the other great modern Swedish players.

One final word on the Hogan waggle. It varied for the type of shot he wanted to hit. As he said in his writing, he never wanted to "groove" his waggle. The waggle also had much more to do with how he wanted to see and feel the approach of his club, hands, and arms into impact than most people realize. This is particularly true of the manner in which he moved his left arm forward (which Carl Welty pointed out to me). Hogan's elbows and arms were always relaxed, and his wrists were flexible. He allowed a little bit of body movement as he waggled the club in preparation for the shot at hand. A flawless waggle.

The preparatory moves. The Hogan grip after 1945 and 1946 changed. Notice the relaxed elbows. The clubhead is now just a few inches off the ground. You can see how beautifully Hogan puts his hands on the club. It is not exaggerated or perhaps as weak as some thought. Hogan said the left-hand grip was in the fingers and palm of that hand. The shaft went diagonally across the hand and under the pad of the thick part of the hand. It did not go up the lifeline. He was emphatic about the pressure points, and this is something I work on endlessly with my students. The first two pressure points are in the back three fingers of the left hand and the middle two fingers of the right hand. The third pressure point is between the left thumb and the lifeline of the right hand, the major connection point of the two hands. In addition to these three main focal or pressure points, Hogan also mentioned that his right pinkie finger hooked around the left forefinger. It did not ride on top of the left forefinger, which is classically called the "Vardon grip." Hogan wrote that he was the only one he knew who used this grip, which can rightfully be called the "Hogan grip." Later Ken Venturi would adapt this grip and teach it to me and others. Incidentally, Tom Watson looks like he uses the same grip.

Frame 115

The clubhead is now ten inches off the ground as Hogan looks at the target. If you look past his head and compare it to frame 036, notice how high he lifts his body, and also how far he shifts left. The man's head that appeared directly over Hogan's left shoulder in the previous photo is now completely blocked from view. This more or less erect upper body posture is a very important feature of Hogan's setup.

Frame 149

More preparation. Notice Hogan's super-soft arms, and his right leg placed farther apart from his left. Check the man standing behind Hogan with his right hand on his hip. I use him as one of the most important guides for this swing sequence. Remember that this is one swing with no camera movement and a perfect angle. This is how you do research.

Setup Keys

Hogan has now fully taken his address stance. The shaft leans away from the target. The arms are still relaxed, and they form a perfect triangle with the shoulders. The right shoulder is slightly lower than the left. Notice that the right toe is slightly toed or turned out, and the left toe is also turned out a quarter turn. Ken said Hogan used a wider stance when driving than he did for his iron play. You can see that wide 3-wood stance in this photo.

Gardner Dickinson told me that leaning the shaft away from the target is one of the best ways to avoid a hook. I used to ask Gardner a thousand questions a day about Hogan. I'm sure I drove him crazy. Yet he loved to talk about Hogan. So did everyone I ever asked who really understood golf, studied golf, or played golf with Hogan.

FACE-ON VIEW

This picture shows Hogan just before he starts his swing away from the ball. The moment is at the completion of his pre-shot routine, setup, and waggle and just at the beginning of the transition into his backswing. Hogan is in a perfect setup position, ready to initiate his swing movement.

Here is a sort of checklist of items in Hogan's completed setup, working from the ground up. It will be followed by a kind of shorthand, frame-by-frame analysis of Hogan's full driver swing:

- The feet are set wide with the instep even with the middle of each shoulder.
- The left foot is flared out toward the target, the right foot pointing nearly perpendicular to the target line.
- The knees are slightly flexed, the left knee just slightly pointed inward toward the right knee, the right knee cocked toward the left knee and slightly forward toward the ball.
- The hips are square to the target line with a slight inclination, the left hipbone tilted higher than the right a few degrees above horizontal toward the target.
- The angle of the spine is tilted 10 degrees away from the target.
- The body tilts away from the target and matches the shoulders, with the left shoulder higher than the right.
- There is a definite cup in the left wrist, while the right wrist is almost flat.
- The right hand is well over the left thumb and on top of the shaft.
- The right elbow is slightly bent.

Last, I want to point out something you might miss. That is, with the shaft leaning back away from the target, the grip will appear stronger. The farther you move the shaft forward the weaker it will appear.

Frame 240

Hogan's chin is just beginning to turn slightly to the right, and his body is just beginning to rock away from the target. The rotation of the chin was definitely a swing trigger for Hogan, as it was for Jack Nicklaus. However, remember both Hogan and Nicklaus were left-eye dominant (so is Tiger Woods). The drift to the right at the beginning of Hogan's swing is something almost every teacher and writer has mis-read. Hogan took the club away with the big muscles, not just the hands. He wrote that there is a slight lateral move of the hips on the backswing.

The Swing

Step 1. Initiating the Swing

The head of the man behind Hogan is now obscured by Hogan's continued movement away from the ball. Look back at frames 230 and 240 and you can clearly see the lateral head sway. Notice, too, that the clubhead has not moved.

In my many rounds of golf with Ken Venturi, he did the exact same lateral move. Once again, the Ben Hogan influence! Ken played, practiced, and copied many Hogan attributes. Other great ball strikers with this early drift include Tom Weiskopf, Angel Cabrera, Anthony Kim, Dustin Johnson, Rory McIlroy, and the younger Tiger Woods.

Frame 261

Hogan's slight drag takeaway is now obvious. Hands and body first. The body moving the club. There is no independent arm and hand movement. No early wrist set. Ken described it as a "paintbrush idea," meaning that it was as if Hogan were painting the ground with his clubhead as the paintbrush. I use it with students who have trouble lagging the club in the downswing, because this body-oriented beginning of the backswing lag actually helps facilitate the proper downswing lag later in the swing. Again, the arms and shoulders initiate the start back, not the clubhead. The last thing to move is the clubhead.

The rocking into the right side is very obvious here. The clubshaft remains between the arms. It appears that Hogan definitely has more weight into the right leg and the clubhead has only moved four or five inches.

Frame 269

This is a major lateral move into a right leg brace. The clubhead can stay very low along the ground doing this. It's great for developing width. Clearly, Hogan did not set the club early or reverse pivot as some say he did.

Frame 270

The clubshaft matches up with the right leg at this stage and is still low to the ground. Notice how much Hogan has moved his head away from the target; there is obvious lateral head movement. Look at the background from the setup photos. Hogan described this initial one-piece move as the first crossroads in the golf swing. On the basis of my extensive work with Ken, I use this as Step 1, or Position 1, in my eight-step swing system.

Frame 274

The clubhead is just now getting off the ground. There is great width. There is hardly any clubface roll, very different from the exaggerated waggle, because it was a "miniature" full swing and would show an open clubface and not a square one as it appears here. Hogan never wanted to feel that clubface shut at any point of his swing. The end of his waggle closely resembles the more open clubface position as he begins to make his move on the downswing and approach to the ball. Therefore one would say that at this point in Hogan's back-swing, the clubface isn't yet open.

Frame 276

Step 2. Extending the Backswing

Look at the space between Hogan's right arm and body. You can see a sliver of white between the right arm and the right side of his body. The wrists beginning to set naturally. The right elbow is not pinned to his body, which is an old and obviously incorrect myth about Hogan's backswing.

Frame 281

Here you really see width in the backswing. Again, there is space between the right elbow and the body, and this represents a critical motion in Hogan's swing in the late 1940s. He is really loading the right side, a phenomenal power move. This is another important checkpoint position I worked on with Carl Welty. He noticed that when the hands got above the knee all of the great ball strikers had the right arm above the left, again indicative of how Hogan turned everything back and away from the ball from the beginning of his swing all in a one-piece motion. This, then, becomes Step 2, a key checkpoint in my teaching system.

Hogan said that by turning the shoulders in unison with the movement of the arms and club you increase the width of your arc. You can see this clearly above.

Also notice that there is only a slight bend in his right arm at the elbow, another sign of his great extension. There is no independent lifting of the club with his right arm whatsoever.

A quarter of the way back the wrists have not yet cocked. Hogan said that there is "no conscious cocking of the wrists at any time." "The cocking of the wrist is gradual as you proceed with the backswing," he said. In Homer Kelley's book *The Golfing Machine* this is called "Random Loading."

Frame 285

Still not much hand action. The body is coiling and loading strong. Bending of the right elbow is beginning, the right shoulder really starting to turn back and away.

Hogan felt and wrote that the head did not move, but in reality it did. You can easily compare this photo to the first one in this sequence. What really happened was that Hogan kept his head centered on top of his spine. As the coiling spine moves away slightly to the right, Hogan's head moves with the coil, giving it the appearance of moving independently to the right. It didn't. As you can see in these photos, Hogan's head also moves slightly down and away from the target. Interestingly, most current top tour players lower the head in the backswing. This is something I believe you should know.

Frame 289

The right shoulder is going back and out of view. The left knee is breaking in behind the ball. Hogan's weight looks to be very much onto his right side, and very powerful. He will now set his wrists quite fast. Ken Venturi schooled me on the right shoulder going "up and behind the right ear." You can see this move clearly above. Ben Doyle, a well-known authorized instructor of The Golfing Machine, explains that Homer Kelley's definition of the above-mentioned Random Loading mean that the left wrist is set neither early nor late. Rather the wrist set begins near waist height.

Frame 291

The wrists are now setting. This is Step 3 in my eight-step swing analysis. The left arm is parallel to the ground. You can see the letter L formed between the left arm and the shaft. I have used letters to more clearly describe this key position in all of my teaching career: for example, the L-Position, the X-Factor, and the Y-Factor. This is the classic L-Position at three-quarters back, or Step 3 in the eight-step swing. Remember, Hogan said he never consciously made an effort to set his wrists during this backswing. It happened naturally as a result of his body's momentum or pivoting action transferring a swinging motion from his body to his shoulders to his arms and wrists. This is what set the club into the L-Position.

Step 3. X-Factor Coiling and Wrist Cock

The right elbow is folding into the body and down. The club-shaft is now more than a 90 degree angle with the left arm. Hogan set his wrists at different stages of the swing depending on what club he was swinging. For example, he set the wrists later with his driver, as in these photos. For short irons he set the wrists earlier. I think this is the optimum way. In *The Golfing Machine*, early wrist setting is called "Sweep Loading." Hogan did this on short irons. On full power swings he created much more width. Notice his wide stance with the 3-wood here, a stance he also used for his fairway woods. He took a more narrow stance when he played the short irons.

Frame 296

We still see a lot of space between Hogan's knees, indicating lower body resistance. Hogan's left arm stays very straight. At this point his hands are far away from the body, even though his right elbow has naturally bent. This indicates excellent maintenance of width.

Hogan looks so solid here and "stacked on the right side," as I've called it for many years. Some teachers say Hogan was stacked on his left side in the backswing. What do you see? I see just the opposite. Notice how he has rolled off the left foot and the left knee is pointing behind the ball. The ankles and feet will show you weight transfer better than anything.

Frame 304

Perfect. The right knee is flexed slightly and braced. Powerful. He is about to change direction. Hogan is now nearing what he called the second crisis in the golf swing, or the second crossroad: the transition move from backswing into downswing, which we will study and discuss in detail in Step 4. On the next few pages you can observe the great Hogan move.

Frame 309

From frame 304 to this one it is clear that Hogan has started what I call the "forward fall" toward the target as the clubhead still goes back. He has just started leaning left onto a flexed left knee at this stage. At this point in the swing the golfer must not hold back the weight transfer from the back foot to the front foot.

Frame 311

Step 4. Backswing Completion and Transition

The clubhead is still going back while Hogan has reversed the lower body. This is the Venturi "two-way motion" idea that we have discussed endlessly. The club "hangs back" and "loads" in response to the hips (core) reversing direction. Look at that solid left arm and the width it creates. Hogan always swung the driver past parallel, even after the accident and even at a much older age. Again, something many teachers misrepresent is the length of his swing. When I watched Hogan play at Champions he was in his late fifties; his driver swing went past parallel even then. He could still rip the driver.

| Frame 315 |

Hogan is clearly moving toward his target. The left knee is clearly returning left. The right knee is flexed. Teachers mistakenly call this the top of Hogan's backswing, when in reality he had completed his full-body coil several frames before. All of my Hogan teachers were aware that Hogan started forward (or left) while the club was still going back. He did not have a stop to his backswing. Something was always moving, just as you see in any top athlete throwing or hitting for power in any sport.

Hogan wrote that "there must be enough lateral movement to get to the left side." I really emphasized this in the *X-Factor* book and my DVDs. It is so widely misunderstood, the most common mistake being that people believe the turn of the hips should begin immediately at the start of the downswing.

The application of power is not a hurry-up process, it cannot be rushed. This is why the two-way move can be so difficult to master. The tendency is to rush. The key is getting the sequence correct. First comes the fall to the left (as I call it) or the lean to the left with the entire body. Ken Venturi used another key idea here: the left shoulder leaves the chin and stays down, both of which ensure that the left arm begins to swing away from the right shoulder as the downswing begins. Watch the next frames to see Hogan do exactly this move. Venturi taught this to great tour players like John Cook and Tom Watson.

Frame 319

The knees are now level and very flexed. The body has lowered. The shaft has lowered. The arms have lowered. The hands have lowered. Hogan's body is squatting or sitting down. The hips are moving laterally down the target line, which was a crucial move getting Hogan forward to his left side. The clubhead and clubshaft are responding, not initiating, and the wrists remain fully cocked just as they were at the completion of his backswing. From here Hogan can turn his hips absolutely as hard to the left as possible.

Frame 320

Step 5a. Moving into Power Position

The left knee is now over the left foot—a big Hogan key. Ken explained the importance of this move to me, and I use it often in my instruction. It stops the spin-out for almost everyone. The left knee is still very flexed, because as Ken said, if it were snapping straight at this point, the tendency would be to pull or "spin" the golfer out of position too far to the left, and in so doing initiate a premature release of the club that would also almost certainly be delivered into the ball over the top. Instead you can see that the clubshaft still stays way back and almost appears to be on Hogan's neck. This is partially an illusion, but there is no doubt that Hogan lowered and delayed the arms longer than any top player.

Frame 321

An unbelievable photo of Hogan. Special. Beautiful. Dynamic. Awesome. The right elbow has returned to the body. There is great width of the left arm, which is gaining massive momentum going straight downplane. Huge lag! The right shoulder is still high, and the left shoulder is down. The knees now look precisely level.

Frame 324

Notice the massive space between the knees. This is indicative of a great sit-down motion—the lowering motion of great ball strikers. The right heel is still down. Hogan is still maintaining tons of lag in this image. The left knee is over the left foot. With this perfect execution of the sit-down motion, Hogan is making full use of the ground for leverage, he is storing his power by maintaining the angle of his set wrists and the club itself, and he is beginning to instinctively calibrate his timing for the delivery of the golf club into impact.

Frame 326

Step 5b. The On-Line Delivery

The right elbow, the hands, and the right knee all line up, something I have described in the *X-Factor* book, DVDs, and other X-Factor articles. My writing and work on television concerning the power moves and power angles in the golf swing came from reviewing thousands of hours of videotape. No book had ever been written exclusively on body action in the golf swing prior to *The X-Factor*. The first chapter had a photo of me with Ken Venturi. As I have reported, he was a huge influence in all of my teaching. Ken was a golf genius who taught many great players, as well as generously sharing Hogan's knowledge with me.

Frame 329

The right shoulder is now under the left. The right wrist is still cocked. The right knee is kicking in. The left leg is bowed. The hands are almost directly above the ball, but the clubhead is over four feet behind the ball. The right heel is leading the toe, which I use as a true fundamental in *The Eight-Step Swing*. The right heel is coming off the ground.

On a driver swing Hogan wrote that "85% of my weight was on the left side at impact." He put a very big emphasis on the inside portion of the right foot, or the right instep. It was a power move. Hogan wrote that he would consciously push off the right instep for more power.

Frame 330

Step 6. Impact

A millisecond before impact. The Hogan bowed left wrist! You can't get a better view of the supinated left wrist. Compare this image to his setup position. Notice how far forward the hands are at this point before impact. When I watched Jimmy Demaret play and practice at Champions, he definitely had this look. Demaret could bow that left wrist and fade it with power every time. In my research of Hogan it's my guess that he used very much of Bobby Jones and very much of Demaret in his visual training. Then it was combined with his work with Bill Melhorn, Henry Picard, Harry Cooper, Paul Runyan, and Johnny Revolta. Those were, I believe, the models Hogan used to build his game.

Frame 331

Just after impact. The left wrist is still solid. The left leg is bracing. The head stays well behind the ball. The clubshaft already points back between the arms, indicating a full release by Hogan. A line through the center of Hogan's head and down to the ground clearly shows the huge move forward. Only the right shoulder and lower part of the right leg remain behind the head. Awesome.

Frame 334

Step 7a. Post-Strike Movement

This photo shows a fantastic extension of the right arm, with the back of the right wrist down and just beginning to cover up the left wrist. The right foot, right hip, and entire right side are firing toward the target. The left shoulder is now pulling away from the target. Although it is not as apparent from this face-on view, the straight line you can draw from Hogan's right shoulder all the way to the clubhead is what I have called the Power Line. You will see it much better on the down-the-target-line view. If you draw another straight line down from Hogan's head you see that everything is forward of it except the right shoulder and the lower part of the right leg.

Frame 336

Step 7b. Classic Step

The clubhead looks like it is being pulled away from Hogan, and indeed, there is a fantastic and free extension of the club-shaft here at Step 7, or halfway through to the finish. The free-flowing and powerful force of Hogan's swing has been described as a "runaway train" (the great paradox of course being that he completely controlled his action). Notice how Hogan's chin and eyes are just starting to release toward the target.

I taught side by side with "Lighthorse" Harry Cooper (a member of the PGA Hall of Fame) at Westchester Country Club in Rye, New York. Harry would tell me that a good player could sometimes feel the centrifugal force of the clubhead pulling the body and head up and through to the finish. This picture gives me that sense. Cooper played a lot of golf with

Hogan in the early years and watched his progress. Without any doubt Hogan gleaned ideas from his time with Cooper. Cooper was one of the straightest drivers of all time and amassed thirty-six PGA Tour wins. With all of the talk to date of the likes of Sergio Garcia, Colin Montgomerie, and even today's number-one-ranked golfer, Lee Westwood, Harry Cooper may very well be the greatest golfer of all who never won a major.

Frame 339

Notice how wide the clubhead appears. The left arm is still connected but also just about to come flying off the body as Hogan swings into his finish. The left shoulder is gone from this view. The hips are facing the target. We can see how active the Hogan body action is in all of these photos. Hogan said the body propelled the golf club and the hands consciously did nothing. His eyes and head are now turning to pick up the flight of the ball.

I spent some great times with the great Tommy Bolt (another PGA Hall of Famer). Tommy, whom many consider one of the greatest ball strikers ever, copied Hogan's grip and later also taught it to Tom Weiskopf. Bolt stressed the "no-hands feeling" he saw in Hogan. He told me he definitely worked very hard to incorporate this action into his own swing. The body released the club while the hands just held on. Jack Nicklaus refers to this same principle as "passive hands." It stood as one of his major fundamentals, and one he spoke of and taught often in his written or video instruction.

Step 8. Completing the Follow-Through

The eyes and head have fully released. The man with his hand on his hip is almost totally in the picture now, showing you how much lateral motion Hogan makes in the forward move. Teachers or anyone, really, who talks about a quiet body or hitting with the hands never studied Hogan.

Frame 349

The focus here is on Hogan's right knee. Again notice the man with his hand on his hip with the bent left leg. Interestingly, there is a good deal of space between this man's left leg and Hogan's right, whereas if you go back to frame 331, there is no space at all between the two men's legs. What do we learn from this? That Hogan's right leg is very relaxed, which has facilitated a free and almost complete shift of his weight onto his left leg and side. Don't dismiss the importance of this observation.

Frame 366

I love to see how far around the left arm travels. Hogan's back has turned so fully that it is now almost facing the camera. What flexibility! When I worked with Johnny Revolta he emphasized how the left arm worked around the body throughout the entire downswing and right to the finish, just as the above picture shows.

Frame 379

The classic Hogan finish from face-on position. He is at ease and in perfect balance. The clubshaft bisects the back of his head. His weight is virtually fully to the left, with the right toe just barely on the ground. Look also at the clubface at the finish here and notice how it is facing away from the target, indicating the full yet controlled freedom of its motion throughout the swing. Many tour professionals today get the clubface in nearly the same position at the end of their swings.

Interestingly, I've reaffirmed through the years of teaching something Jackie Burke taught me back in my college years at Houston. Going to a great finish position helps many other facets of your swing without conscious thought. Hogan still has the most copied finish in the history of golf. It was the exact finish Johnny Revolta taught. Homer Kelley and Eddie Merrins, "the Little Pro," are two other fine teachers who have emphasized the importance of swinging all the way into a great finish position. This is an idea that truly stands the test of time.

5

Down-the-Target-Line View

The following swing sequence came from film shot in 1947. The down-the-line camera angle is set up perfectly to analyze Hogan's iron shot. This is how I was trained to film, precisely down the target line. Now modern launch monitors like Trackman, which is used on the PGA Tour, do the same. The length of the shaft relative to Hogan's height (and longer-than-normal arms) yields a flatter swing plane. If you look closely in the following photos you will be able to see the ball's low-boring trajectory.

Frame 463

Here is Hogan at the Augusta National Golf Course. The camera is looking straight down his target line. Notice the straight back, with no curve from the tailbone to the section between his shoulder blades. At this point the top of the spine to the head is relaxed, and the line from the center of the shoulders to the top of the head is on an angle. The knees are flexed, the stance is slightly open. You can see just a sliver of Hogan's front leg, indicating that the hips are slightly open, identical to his toe line. This was a point Ken Venturi went over with me time and again. He told me that Hogan paid close attention to the hip line at setup for his preferred shot shape. The feet, knees, hips, and shoulders are all aimed slightly left to accommodate the slight fade he will hit on this swing. Notice the relaxed neck and head. There is nothing rigid or stiff. The arms do not hang straight down, but rather a bit outward. The right arm has a slight bend. The clubshaft points directly at the belt.

I placed a line through the shaft to improve the visual. Line needs to be put in here and several other spots. Hogan recommended practicing your setup and posture at home using a full-length mirror.

Hogan set the right hand very high and very much in the fingers. Every great teacher who actually played with him mentioned this fact to me (Venturi, Gardner Dickinson, Johnny Revolta, Paul Runyan, Claude Harmon, Jackie Burke). The right hand, according to Hogan, was the more difficult hand to position properly. For him, the right-hand grip was instrumental in eliminating the hook.

Frame 493

As the backswing begins we see the clubhead working slightly inside due to the early coil of the shoulders. We can already see Hogan's entire left arm that was totally hidden in the setup. His right shoulder still has not moved upward. We can see the bend in the right arm/elbow joint more clearly here, which he had at setup. Notice how Hogan has already turned his head slightly away from the target, a great move for the left-eye-dominant golfer. Remember, Hogan was left-eye dominant, like Jack Nicklaus and Tiger Woods.

Venturi, Revolta, and Dickinson all emphasized the importance of the takeaway (in my lessons the first crossroad in the golf swing). Hogan learned a part of this from Revolta, and for sure passed it along to Venturi and Dickinson. Hogan believed in a classic one-piece move away from the ball, shoulders leading almost simultaneously, with the arms and hands unified.

Frame 496

Now just a few feet off the ball in what I term Step 1 in my eight-step analysis system, Hogan clearly displays the classic "one-piece takeaway." You can now see this first crossroad move in his golf swing. Since Hogan had only two crossroads, obviously any student of the golf swing should study this image very carefully.

Ken emphasized this part of the swing to all of the top tour players I watched him teach. Over the years he has probably shown me the Hogan takeaway action a thousand times. Ken did it perfectly himself and is one reason Byron Nelson said he was the greatest iron player he ever saw. This takeaway can help every golfer connect and simplify his or her backswing and make it repeatable day after day. As Ken told me, some things stand the test of time. This is one of them, for sure. Sam Snead, Jack Nicklaus, Greg Norman, Byron Nelson, and Tiger Woods are a few examples of great players with the one-piece Hogan takeaway.

Frame 500

Hogan has the clubshaft and clubhead in front of his body. The shaft still points into the body. The knees are still flexed just as they were at address. You can really see the athletic bend in Hogan's knees here outlined in his trousers. The right shoulder begins its upward climb. The shoulders do not turn level but at an angle.

Frame 502

This image is halfway through the backswing, or what I call Step 2 in *The Eight-Step Swing*. This is a classic checkpoint position. For hundreds of years golfers have checked this position to see if the clubshaft is in good position. Ken taught me to hold this position and then turn my body to the camera. If Hogan did this the club would be square and in line, or what Ken said was perfect. It is very important to note the angle of Hogan's shoulders. The right shoulder is climbing and elevating back and around. The left shoulder is lower. Hogan turns his shoulders on a 90-degree angle to his spine, which is obviously tilted forward, toward the ball/target line. Your shoulders do not turn level. Take a look at the lower part of Hogan's sweater showing the angle of the core.

When I worked with Claude Harmon in Palm Springs he had me practice the handshake takeaway with the right hand bending somewhat back upon itself and not frozen stiff. He wanted the right hand in the same position as the clubface at halfway back. We also called this the "toe-up position." Harmon always noted the lateral move Hogan made away from the ball by halfway back.

Frame 510

With the left arm parallel to the ground, Hogan has "set the wrists" and the club has turned upside down. The clubhead is now pointing at the sky. Notice that the left arm is pointing slightly to the right of his target, between 30 and 40 degrees, and has gone against the chest. The clubshaft points almost at the ball/target line. You will want to study this frame carefully because we will use it to compare it against his downswing at the same position. Hogan has the shaft move vertical going back then coming down. I call this Step 3 in *The Eight-Step Swing*, and I note that Hogan is clearly under his famous pane of glass with the right shoulder, the clubshaft, and the hands.

Interestingly, the modern launch monitor used by virtually every tour player is set right down the target line, too. Many teachers film inside the target line, which I feel is far inferior; you cannot see the ball flight. It is almost impossible to do on-course video instruction unless you film down the target line. Carl Welty has the most extensive video library in the world, all shot precisely the same way. That's how you do great research. That's how you compare swings accurately.

Frame 522

Here you clearly see one of the two Hogan "secrets" he put into his swing in 1946. One of the game-changers was the "slight cupping of the left wrist in the backswing." Study this picture, paying close attention to his left wrist. Combined with the slightly weaker left hand, Hogan's swing became hook-proof. Notice here how his left arm and his shoulder plane nearly match up. Hogan has loaded his left arm "low," not really flat. It's a feeling of keeping the left arm in and "connected to the body," as Jimmy Ballard would explain in his teachings. At this section of the swing the clubshaft is in perfect position. Hogan's elbows are nearly level.

Frame 524

Reaching the top of the backswing, Hogan is about to reverse directions with his lower body. Again Ken described this to me as Hogan's "two-way" swing action. Something is always moving. There's no stop at the top. You can see a small space between the legs, clearly indicating that Hogan's left knee has moved both back and out toward the ball. His left wrist is now almost flat with just the slightest of cup. The right elbow is in close to the body and the right forearm is pointing down as the reversal of swing direction is taking place. The left arm and shoulders are aligned. The right knee is still flexed. As Hogan reaches the top of his backswing you can see the position of his right hand. The right wrist is bent back just as it would to throw a rock far out into a lake.

Hogan used the right hand and the right arm as his guide for the backswing. Few people know this, and nobody has written about it. I know this from my detailed communications with Jackie Burke and Ken Venturi. That's a big clue to slotting the backswing time after time. Your right hand gets in a throwing position. Starting in 1946, Hogan felt he could slot his backswing every time.

Frame 530

This is near the very end of the backswing. The clubshaft is just short of parallel. This is the second crossroad in the swing. Although you cannot see it from this view, Hogan is now leaning forward toward the target. His head has dropped some more—check his eye position with the tree line. This is the start of dropping the club into the "slot." When after Tiger Woods hits an off-line shot commentators mention that it's because he has dropped down I cringe. That's not why it went off-line. Tiger has had that drop and sit-down action his entire life. Most great ball strikers do in the backswing and almost every single one on the downswing. The sit-down is a key move in any great swing.

Frame 532

Hogan's clubshaft is still going back, meaning his wrists continue to cock, while you see clear evidence of the legs and hips turning back to the target. Ken told me that Hogan's club hung in the air for a split second as the body changed direction. That lower body initiation greatly encourages the drop-off of the shaft (more laid off). This photo shows the very beginning of the hips moving laterally and the result of perfect lower body action. You see that Hogan is lowering into what Sam Snead described in his own swing as a "squat."

I've written extensively about this squat or sit-down movement that top ball strikers make. I described it in the *X-Factor* book and then better in the *X-Factor* DVD produced in 2004. In the DVD I used the term "compression," meaning the body compresses downward. I write about this move in *The Eight-Step Swing* as well. Again, I did not invent this idea, but rather studied it extensively on videotape and computer clips. Recently, I've heard many commentators use my compression lingo.

Frame 538

Hogan is now in transition mode, which I call Early Step 5. You can see how the left arm has lowered under the shoulder plane. The legs are flexed and stable. Again, I call it compression, which you will see even more at the impact picture. This idea is something that great ball strikers achieve for power. It's a natural athletic move, but in higher-handicap golfers it is infrequent or never comes close to happening. Hogan's knees are equally flexed. You can see the downward push of the legs, especially the right leg as he has recentered his weight.

Frame 540

Hogan said he wanted his arms in close to the body in the downswing. This is the opposite of what many amateurs do when they start the downswing. Hogan's hands are still positioned behind him.

Frame 544

The clubshaft is now on a significantly lower plane than the backswing. The clubshaft now points outside ball/target line. Looking directly down the target line, Hogan's shaft is perfect. It bisects the right shoulder and the right elbow. This is an excellent checkpoint for your swing. Remember to have your camera directly on the target line and at least eight yards behind the ball. Notice that Hogan's knees are parallel to the target line at this point of the swing.

The knees parallel (at Early Step 5 when the clubshaft is almost halfway down) is something Claude Harmon showed me in my lessons with him. He would lay a shaft across my thighs. He wanted to make sure you were not spinning out. If you did, the shaft across the thighs would be pointed left. Hogan's shoulders are nearly level again.

Frame 548

Hogan is pouring on the power. The right knee is kicking outward past the ball. The left leg is now clearly visible. The left hip is not moving laterally but instead on an angle. Both hips are rising. The right elbow is very near the right hip, in front of but not touching the body. It's very interesting to compare this picture with Hogan's backswing picture at the same point. Again notice the significant lowering of the head and the massive change of the right arm and elbow. Hogan is definitely pushing off the right foot, and the right knee is obviously kicking forward. You can see a wide gap between the arms that will quickly close by impact. Hogan's hips are far ahead of his shoulders. The hips are 30 degrees open while the shoulders are now just about parallel to the target line. Everything is unwinding at an incredible speed, and the club is right on what I call the Power Line.

Frame 552

Impact, the moment of truth. A perfect picture to compare with Hogan's setup position. We see that nothing is the same, except that Hogan has returned the clubshaft almost exactly to its position at setup. Compare the shaft plane line I drew here with the shaft plane line from setup. Add the line The shaft angle at setup and at impact are almost exactly the same. There is just a bit of air under that right heel, but Hogan is clearly pushing off. The belt line is clearly tilted. I measured this at 48 degrees from horizontal. Again, check to see that Hogan's head has lowered a significant amount. Check this against his address position. "Compression"—it's a power move used by most great ball strikers hitting iron shots. I always look at and compare the right ear at setup versus impact. The body has lowered to the maximum, allowing Hogan to drive the club longer and lower down the target line.

Frame 554

A millisecond after impact. The right heel is clearly off the ground. The hands and arms are in close to the body. Hogan returns the hands and shaft low. You get the feeling of "down and left." Obviously the bow of his left wrist makes it possible to hit extremely long and powerful golf shots.

Frame 556

The ball is just now exploding off the clubface. The entire left side of Hogan's trunk is visible. The hips are rotated almost 90 degrees. The shoulders are closing fast, meaning they have almost caught up with the hips. The shoulders are extremely left and open, which is a key move in the "big muscle swing." The hands are in close to the body, and you get the sense that everything is going left. I also get the sense of no flip of the wrists. That is a trademark of the Hogan swing.

Jackie Burke gave me a tremendous image for achieving this goal. He said, "Visualize you are standing on a sheet of ice and the bottom of your club has a nail in it. Simulate yourself at impact with your hands ahead of the clubhead, but with the nail firmly on the ice. Now drag the nail left after impact." That's exactly what I see Hogan doing in this picture.

Frame 560

This is something I wrote about in the first edition of *The Eight-Step Swing*. At this point in the swing you see "no hands and no club"! That means the clubshaft has swung back to the left and is now directly in front of Hogan and therefore invisible to the camera from this angle. Remember, the camera is set perfectly down the line. Notice the ball rocketing toward the target, and how Hogan's head and eyes are already rotating to pick up its flight. I also like to study his foot action. From this angle we see significant air under the right heel.

Frame 568

My students are often surprised when I show them how far left the pros swing the club after impact. Many have the idea of "swinging at the target" or "swinging down the line." There is no line. The clubhead swings on an arc, not down the target line. Hogan's shaft matches up with his downswing plane pointing again just outside his original ball/target line.

Frame 576

I love this picture. The upper body is still angled. The line from the top of Hogan's head to his tailbone is perfect. The right arm is angled precisely on the same plane angle as the left arm was in the backswing. The left elbow (forearm) points down. Again, this is a major key in Hogan's technique and is important for great ball striking: cup in the left wrist, flat right wrist. This follow-through was such a significant part of Hogan's swing shape. The wrist and arm match up. The hips are pointing left of the target. I've seen many of my low-handicap students and tour players hit shots with a restricted punch finish just like the photo above. Again we see that long right arm of Hogan. Certainly a trademark move.

Frame 596

As Tiger Woods continued to work on his golf swing it was obvious to any instructor that he copied the Hogan move past impact and into the finish. If you compare Tiger (circa 2005 to 2009) to this photo the image would be almost identical to Ben Hogan. Tiger, like many others, has modeled many parts of his swing technique on Hogan.

Frame 634

Hogan's finish appears a bit high because the camera was set low for this picture. However, it is definitely a high finish, indicating that he "held off" this shot to ensure a fade. Notice that he is fully over to the left side with his right toe balanced on the ground. The clubshaft points diagonally at the target line. There is lots of cupping in Hogan's left wrist, along with a cup in his right as well.

I will never forget the effort Johnny Revolta placed in this type of finish. He wanted those hands far to the left side of the head just like this photo shows. I can't help but think that Hogan picked up some of his famous finish from Revolta. I always look at the clubface at the finish of the swing. Hogan wanted the clubface in this position, pointing at the camera and with the toe down.

6

Forty-Five-Degree-Angle View

This sequence shows Ben Hogan from a front camera angle hitting a driver off the tee while playing in the 1948 Masters. His pre-shot routine is not shown here. The photo sequence begins just as he is set to begin his backswing motion.

Frame 000

Notice the black baseball cap. He never wore one after 1950. It must have been a bright, sunny day, as indicated by all of those sunglasses in the crowd. Yet Hogan is wearing a sweater, and the gallery has warm clothing too. Those early spring days can be pretty cool at Augusta, and the weather at the Masters is generally pretty unpredictable.

Look how Hogan's right arm hangs out and away from his body, very much unlike the drawings in *Five Lessons* on page 49, the ones with the rope tying his arms together. This rope image described what Hogan felt rather than the actual orientation of his arms at address. (However, not all of the drawings of Hogan's setup are incorrect in *Five Lessons*.) You can see how much on top of his left hand he places his right hand.

Frame 032

Hogan cocks the chin away from the target. This was part of the ignition system that helped get his swing started. One of his nicknames during this part of his career was "the Mighty Atom." This turn of the chin is a natural move as the shoulders turn. Hogan, like Jack Nicklaus, turned the chin even before takeaway. It was part of his pre-shot routine and/or preparatory moves as well.

Frame 038

The clubhead starts away super low. The clubface appears to open from this view, though it is actually staying square to the curving backswing arc. The body, shoulders, and arms dominate at this early start-up stage of the swing.

The clubhead is just a few inches farther away. The right shoulder is moving out of sight and back very early. This indicates a one-piece takeaway with the hands, arms, club, and upper body all in sync.

Frame 041

The right shoulder is gone from view, indicating lots of early turn. You can see the wide extension of his arms. Notice the gallery. Nothing has changed. Everyone is super-still.

Frame 042

The hips are beginning to turn. But the lower body is very stable and very balanced. The feet appear quiet.

Frame 044

Notice the creases in Hogan's sweater. This indicates serious upper-body coil.

Frame 045

The creases are more apparent in his slacks. The entire body is now coiling. You can now easily see the tilt of the shoulders. The right shoulder is moving up and behind the right ear.

Look at how far his left arm moves away from the target, carrying the left shoulder with it. The left arm appears very straight, too.

Frame 049

It's very important to note the position of the clubshaft here. Many teachers have said that Hogan swung on one plane back and through. We'll see if that's true. Notice how the shaft is just under the neck of the man wearing sunglasses in the background, whom we will refer to again shortly. The left knee is breaking outward and behind the ball.

Frame 050

The clubshaft and shoulders match up from this view at this stage. Notice the left foot rolling inward. Just by looking at this image one feels that Hogan is very coiled and very powerful. He establishes resistance with his lower body, but he certainly has turned those hips.

Frame 051

The left heel is now slightly off the ground, a point many teachers miss. Notice Hogan's hands now just on the man's chin in the background.

Frame 054

Hogan's huge power coil. Look at the stretch in his sweater and slacks. You can see his back right buttock and right leg, indicating that he has turned and coiled his left side into the brace of his right leg and hip. Look at his rolled left ankle and left foot. This very clearly indicates that he has shifted the majority of his weight off of that foot and onto his right side. So much for those who said Hogan "reverse pivoted," keeping a great deal of weight on his left leg during the backswing. The clubhead is well past parallel and pointing pretty much at the target.

Hogan has obviously changed direction, as his left foot/ heel is starting to plant into the ground. The clubhead is still going back, Hogan's body beginning to move forward. This is the famous Hogan two-way action.

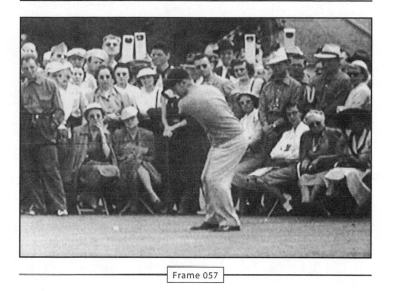

Frame 057

A beautiful sit-down move by Hogan, indicated by the fact that both of his knees are bent. You can now see his right knee. The feet are flat down on the ground. The body has lowered. You can see how much the shaft has laid down on a lower plane, as it now intersects the left shoulder of the man behind him and is nowhere near his neck anymore. There are two planes in Hogan's swing. One going up and one coming down. See frame 059.

Frame 059

Remember frame 050? If not, go back and look again. Hogan's shaft has lowered to a much different level and is much more horizontal than it was there. The hips are unwinding at super-high speed. The arms are just responding to the lowering of the body. Again, this is the classic "sit-down position." Hogan is clearly lower than his address position. From here he will fire through the shot, and as he does the left hip will rise dramatically.

Frame 060

Entering the impact zone. I call this the delivery position. The hips are way left, and due to their activity and the width of his driver stance the right heel is already coming off the ground. Hogan, Sam Snead, Nicklaus, and the modern greats talk about power coming out of the right instep.

Frame 061

A millisecond before impact. The right heel is three to four inches off the ground. The hips are almost facing the target. Notice how much lower Hogan's head is now compared to how it was in the setup position. A huge power move. Ed Dudley, the former president of the PGA, was quoted as saying, "Hogan is one of the longest hitters the game has ever known." This may surprise some readers.

Smash. You can see the athleticism. You can almost feel the impact. The right heel is now four or five inches off the ground. Hogan has written about how his right leg and knee are very relaxed at this point, having already powerfully pushed off. Now the right leg simply slides forward toward the left leg. The left knee has gone from very flexed to bowed. See how the left foot has rolled. Hogan's weight is obviously on his left side. Although blurred, the left wrist still looks solid.

Frame 064

The entire left side is stretching up. The club is released with the hips and the body, not the hands. Hogan said the hands consciously do nothing. The right shoulder is moving through hard, having already turned Hogan's head to the left, preparing to track the flight of the ball. This is a modern move for great ball striking. Notice the left elbow riding close to the body, moving left as the body continues to turn left past impact. This was an idea copied by a great player I worked with and learned from named Doug Sanders. Doug was a great shotmaker on the PGA Tour and won twenty times. He was a great student of the golf swing and copied many Hogan moves. Doug, like other great players I've mentioned in this book, hit millions of practice shots holding this post-impact position. Obviously they were small shots and done with a short iron, but this picture of Hogan was the position Doug held with those short practice shots. In fact, in addition to his flashy style of dress and outgoing personality, Doug was best known for his very short swing, back and through. If you get a chance to see old footage of his swing (and it was a great one!), you'll notice that some swings actually ended or ceased their motion just about at the position Hogan is here in this picture. Sometimes the practice routines of great players work so well that they build them right into the swings they make in competition. All golfers can learn something from this.

Doug Sanders is also remembered for the small putt he missed to win the British Open in St. Andrews, Scotland, outright. (He often says in interviews that he's able to forget about that putt for ten or fifteen minutes each day.) He lost that tournament in a playoff to Jack Nicklaus.

Frame 065

The left shoulder is pulling around hard. The hips are now well left of the target. Notice the line of buttons running up the center of Hogan's sweater. This shows very precisely the angle of his spine tilt at this stage of the swing. Hogan's hip line is way up, five to six inches higher than at its sit-down point. Notice the lady in the background with sunglasses just above Hogan's left hip and compare this view to the previous pictures. Observe how much closer to her chin his left hip now appears than in the other photos.

Frame 066

Hogan's left elbow is down and has started to fold or bend, and his right wrist is flat. The right arm is crossing under the shoulders. The right wrist flat means the left wrist must have some cup on its back at this stage of the swing. In other words, the left wrist does not stay bowed or flat into the finish.

Frame 067

Hogan's eyes are fully tracking the drive, which no doubt resembles a bullet. Notice the bow in his body created by his full push of the hips, and his steady head. His weight is now toward the heel of the left foot, and, again, his hips are also much higher than at their low point in the sit-down position of his downswing.

Frame 070

The right arm is now elevating dramatically, indicating much more of an arm release than a hands release.

Frame 072

Notice how close together the elbows look from this angle. The right shoulder is high and forward toward the target. The left shoulder is well around and back.

Frame 076

The all-time classic finish. The clubshaft appears to run through Hogan's ears. The knees are close together. Perfect balance. The lady in black in the background is now fully visible (refer to frame 054, where Hogan's full backswing coil blocks out the left half of her body), indicating that Hogan has continued to turn all the way through the shot well past impact. Notice how tall he is at the finish.

7

Left-Handed Swing
Sequence with Analysis

'm including the following left-handed sequence for a couple
of reasons, not the least of them being that I thought it
would be cool to look at Ben Hogan's swing from a different
perspective. Of course, I'm well aware that there are many left-
handed golfers in the world (some may be surprised to learn
that when Hogan was a young boy he began by swinging left-
handed but switched to right-handed because it was easier to
find good right-handed golf clubs), so perhaps this chapter is
especially for them. We shouldn't forget that Phil Mickelson,
naturally a right-handed person, learned to play lefty because
he would try to mimic his father, a righty, who would train
young Phil by swinging in front of him and having Phil swing

as well—left-handed. And then there's PGA legend Johnny Bulla, a great friend who had seven top five finishes in major championships, including a runner-up finish in the Masters and two runner-up finishes in the British Open, but perhaps even more remarkably, thanks to his ambidexterity, broke his course record of 62 at Papago, achieved right-handed, but later broke it again shooting a 61 left-handed. To him I dedicate this chapter.

The sequence of photos is consistent with the eight steps I use to analyze the swing of my own students and the best players in the world. In each of the positions in the sequence, including the address position, I can tell you that Hogan is absolutely perfect. Use these positions to understand more about control, accuracy, and power.

The eight photos here are the in-swing steps, to which I usually give the following labels:

Step 0. Address

Step 1. The takeaway

Step 2. Halfway back

Step 3. Three-quarter backswing completion

Step 4. Top of the backswing

Step 5. Move down to the ball

Step 6. Impact

Step 7. Post-impact extension and early follow-through

Step 8. Swing finish and rebound

Note: I always use the setup as a key position, but not an in-swing position. We will study Hogan's setup from different views. In Steps 5 and 7, I use two checkpoints. This gives my instructors, in fact, twelve key checkpoints and places to stop video review.

Step 0. Address

The fundamental in my mind is a great setup. Left-handers have a huge disadvantage due to few great photos of the great ball strikers at setup. Look at those soft arms! Just the opposite of the illustrations in *Five Lessons*. Copy this setup and not those.

Step 1

Step 1. The Takeaway

Hogan called this the first of the two crossroads in the swing. It is of one piece with shoulders, arms, hands, and club all together. Notice that Hogan's chin points to the back foot. This is extremely important for a full, powerful coil.

Step 2

Step 2. Halfway Back

Notice the slight rotation of Hogan's head. He is loading away from the target and in the direction of the club. Notice the space between the arms. The left arm is above the right arm. The left leg is braced. These are key ideas for lefties to see.

Step 3. Three-Quarter Backswing Completion

Notice how Hogan has set the wrists from Step 2. He has achieved the classic L-Position. His weight is moving clearly off the right instep. The right knee is just beginning to be pulled by the coil. The left side is beautifully stacked and loaded.

Step 4

Step 4. Top of the Backswing

The right knee has moved behind the ball, but Hogan's body is already falling (or transitioning) forward. See the man with the cap in the background. (Also remember that these photos of Hogan were taken off film, so the camera was shooting action shots of one swing. There are no camera tricks.) I call this the "fall forward." This is the very earliest stage.

Step 5. Move Down to the Ball

Hogan rotates the right knee over the right foot. Very athletic and responsive. The left elbow is tight to the body. A beautiful sit-down move and massive lag.

Step 6

Step 6. Impact

The front leg braces and begins to straighten. This is a major power move. There's air under the left heel. The left hand is in front of the left toe. The left forearm explodes, providing major thrust into the impact zone. The man in the background with his legs crossed provides a great background for showing Hogan's lateral motion. Of course the famous bowed lead wrist is very evident. Hogan wrote extensively on this subject.

Step 7

Step 7. Post-Impact Extension and Early Follow-Through

Notice the bow in Hogan's body due to a huge hip thrust. The right arm is thrown off the body. It explodes off the body. Phenomenal extension. Perfect release of the arms. The right shoulder continues to move with the club.

Step 8

Step 8. Swing Finish and Rebound

The all-time classic finish. It's great for everyone to copy. Isn't it interesting to compare Hogan's relaxed left leg and knee to the man with the crossed legs directly behind him? The foot and leg closely match up. Very relaxed indeed!

8

Hogan's Practice Routines and Drills

Ben Hogan believed in and put into practice the idea of copying the form and techniques of other top golfers to improve his game. I was taught to do the same thing by Jackie Burke, Ken Venturi, Al Mengert, Bob Toski, Claude Harmon, Harry Cooper, and other great teachers/players. I teach "golf moves," and one important and effective way I do this is by demonstrating a move myself or by using a pro example. Any pro example can usually work for most amateurs, but Hogan is still perhaps the best model. Very early in his training he copied the swing technique and golf movements of Ed Stewart, a good amateur golfer at Glen Garden Golf Club. Hogan caddied for Stewart and credited him in *Five Lessons*. An early example how Stewart's swing helped Hogan's was Hogan's improved left knee movement. Hogan said his knee shot straight out on the backswing while Stewart's broke in nicely to the right. Hogan made this observation when he was still a young caddy, then began to work this improved knee action into his own swing.

However, no matter how closely Hogan observed and learned from others, and considering his legendary and prodigious practice sessions, he didn't get stuck on swing mechanics or technique as even some top professionals do today. He played the game.

Jackie Burke wrote in his notes to me, "Ben Hogan before the war and after his accident was always the same. He never looked backwards in his endeavor to play golf. He played the game for the moment and the way he saw the game. He was a visionary person who saw every shot before making any swing. Looking at scoreboards was not his game. He focused on the now."

I use one of Hogan's famous training drills described in *Five Lessons* in my teaching. It works wonders. Hogan demonstrated his drill on *The Ed Sullivan Show* in the mid-1960s. The idea is to start with small, connected swings and build the motion into a bigger swing. Hogan showed how the arms tie into the torso and how the legs, feet, and big muscles move the golf club, and he demonstrated this for the television audience by holding his arms tightly against the right and left sides of his torso while he gripped a golf club in his hands. He executed the drill by simply making a gentle and small turning or pivoting motion with his body along with a small weight shift from his front foot to his back, then reversing the shaft from the back foot to the front. Viewers could easily see Hogan's body, arms, and club, and again, how all were tied in together and everything moved both rhythmically and smoothly.

In his writings Hogan also compared the golf swing to that of an infielder in baseball. To quote him from *Five Lessons*, "In general character, the correct motion of the right arm and hand in the impact area resembles the motion an infielder makes when he throws half sidearm, half under handed to first after fielding a ground ball."

Hogan loved baseball. How do I know? It is documented, but the real way I know is through my great friend Ralph Terry. Ralph pitched for the New York Yankees and was the MVP of the 1961 World Series. He won three games in a seven-game series, winning the final game 1–0. The year before, Ralph threw one of the most memorable pitches in World Series history when Bill Mazeroski of the Pittsburgh Pirates hit an unlikely home run in the bottom of the ninth inning, causing the Yankees to lose the series. It was the one and only time Ralph worked as a reliever.

Ralph, a terrific golfer who would even play on the Champions Senior Tour, met Hogan at Shady Oaks when Ralph was still playing in the major leagues. Ralph sat down with his hosts that day, Hogan and Ted Weiner, a good friend of Hogan's and a member of Shady Oaks. Ralph told me that Hogan knew a lot about baseball and of course knew very well that Ralph played on a team that included Mickey Mantle and Roger Maris. However, Hogan was mainly interested in Ted Williams. That was his favorite player. Later, as Ralph played other times at Shady Oaks, Hogan would encourage Ralph to tell him the same Ted Williams stories he had already told him. Ralph said Hogan's quote was, "I always fancied Ted Williams's swing."

Sam Byrd, another former Yankee, showed Hogan a drill he observed Babe Ruth use for working on his hitting. He placed a handkerchief under Hogan's left armpit. Byrd wanted that handkerchief to stay glued to the armpit. It was particularly good for the one-piece takeaway and the feel of connection through the impact zone. Hogan would use this idea his entire career. My friend and famous golf teacher Jimmy Ballard was taught by Byrd and used this idea in his teaching as a mainstay, while giving it the name "connection." Now many teachers use the Ballard "connection" idea and the drill Byrd showed Ballard from which it was derived. The drill Hogan used on *The Ed Sullivan Show* was very close to the teaching of connection on which Ballard would expound when I worked with him in Pell City, Alabama, in the late 1970s. Connection unites, integrates the motion and action of the knees, hips, and arms into a beautiful blend. We also call it syncing, and the drill of placing a handkerchief, a golf glove, or a small towel under the left armpit while making practice swings or even hitting balls will help golfers improve this important aspect of the swing, as it did for Hogan. It's an idea copied by many current top teachers and is an excellent one for you to try.

Hogan learned the many functions of the "waggle" from Johnny Revolta. He watched and observed Revolta as he changed his waggle for various shots. It's important to note that Hogan let the club waggle over the top of and past the ball. Stopping the waggle at the ball as so many golfers do introduces the danger of training the hands to stop too quickly, thus decelerating the club before impact during actual swings.

Claude Harmon was the head professional at Winged Foot when I came to New York to begin teaching at Westchester Country Club. I became good friends with Lex Alexander, then the teaching assistant for Claude. We played a lot of golf at Winged Foot and discussed the teachings of Claude in detail. I also took a few lessons from Claude at Winged Foot and watched him teach often. Later I would meet him for lunch each week and also take more lessons when I was the director of golf at Tamarisk Country Club. Claude was then teaching across the street at Morningside Country Club. He told me about Hogan's routine at Seminole Golf Club, which Hogan often played just prior to the Masters. On certain days, from 9 a.m. to noon he would slice 3-irons the entire time. That was a staple of Hogan's practice. Claude told me Hogan hit big slices, guaranteeing that the dreaded hook would never show up. He hit all types of shots and all clubs but would do heavy fade/cut practice as a vital part of his practice regimen. From noon to 1 p.m. he ate lunch. At 1 p.m. he teed off, many times with Claude. Claude was proud to say he shot a 61 playing with Hogan.

Hogan had two other favorite exercises. One was to squeeze a towel for hand strength. The other was to set the club down at address and pick it up with the wrists, which strengthened the precise hand and wrist muscles used in gripping the club throughout the swing. One should not move the arms or body as the wrists move up and down. There is no rolling of the wrists during this exercise, and this shows how the cocking and uncocking of the left wrist controls or moves the clubhead only, not the clubface. The clubface remains square.

Hogan showed a drill in *Five Lessons* where he placed a clubshaft against his right leg. He wanted the right leg to be the brace of his backswing. Ken Venturi always emphasized to me this idea of a braced right leg accepting the weight transfer in the backswing without sliding. Ken actually wore a right shoe that was modified. He had the shoe built with an insole that sloped or angled inward. This helped him to avoid any move to the outside of the right foot, and helped him brace the right side à la Hogan. Hogan, as many know, wore an additional spike on his right shoe.

Another Hogan drill I use often is the halfway-down check swing. Hogan did this with the right thumb and forefinger off the shaft. He did not ever want pressure on those two points that activate the top tendon in the right forearm. If you make that mistake you greatly encourage coming over the top, or over the shaft plane, by overengaging the right hand, right arm, and shoulder.

Last, I must write that many of Hogan's practice ideas I have read about in other books were pure fabrication. I've read where Hogan hit a prescribed series of shots each day. Not one of his playing partners or his good friends ever mentioned this to me, or they denied it when I asked them if it were true. So this tells me that much of what you read about Hogan's practice is just a flat-out lie. It didn't happen. What I disclose to you in these pages are the real facts of how Hogan practiced and perfected his swing. Nothing is made up.

Conclusion

B en Hogan had a gift for describing and writing about his golf swing. It's a rare great player in any sport who can teach their technique or fundamentals or write about them, but Hogan could and did both.

Still, the ideas and observations I made through his friends and contemporaries, plus the research I've done, showed me that some of the contents of *Five Lessons* did not describe or show what Hogan really did in his swing, and I've pointed out a few of the illustration errors in that book.

The drawings were intended to describe "feel." Yet it is the motion picture photography you've just studied in this book that actually shows what Hogan did. When writing about the golf swing, the task is to link up or match what really happens during the swing to the way the swing subjectively feels to the teacher or, in Hogan's case, the player doing the writing. Remember, feel is important. It might be the most important key to playing golf. What Hogan wrote might not look exactly the way he felt it, but how he felt his swing was completely "correct" for him.

This describes exactly why writing about the golf swing from an overly scientific perspective is often self-defeating, and might actually become a swing killer.

There is unquestionably a geometry and science in a great golf swing. Focusing only on detailed and prescribed movements is almost always disastrous, because it quite literally loses sight of the swing as a whole. Instead, it is the integration or blending of the motion, or what I call the golf moves, into your game that enables you to reach your potential as a golfer. Like learning dance steps, getting the feel of the moves and movements is immensely important. Just having someone scientifically write out the moves and then asking students to follow them mechanically is an extremely weak way to learn to dance. Being able to write out a dance step perfectly does not mean the writer can do that step. Conversely, not being able to write it out oneself does not mean you cannot do it. The same holds true for leaning to consistently execute great golf swings. The capacity to do so requires a blend of understanding what a great swing consists of in the first place through a visual picture.

We are not machines and can't simply be programmed to make great golf swings every time. Even Homer Kelley's book *The Golfing Machine* is only a metaphor or comparison using difficult and sometimes inaccurate engineering terms, suggesting that with the complete scientific knowledge of correct swing mechanics—and a lot of practice, of course—golfers can approach true consistency *as if* they were machines. In other words, regardless of how accurately or insightfully the teachers or players writing instructional material describe the swing and/or instruct the reader or student on how to execute the moves they are teaching, they simply cannot *feel* a good swing for the student. Registering and remembering those subjective feels in their own body as they swing remains the critical responsibility of each golfer, and Hogan knew this well.

I'm someone who believes in seeing the whole motion of the golf swing and then breaking it down into building blocks that are manageable for my students to understand and execute. Use this book as a guide to do exactly that. Use it as something to visualize both the parts of the swing, while always striving to integrate those parts into one complete motion. You can indeed use it to work on small segments of your swing. Oftentimes a swing drill specific to your needs will work well.

I cannot imagine any golfer who would not be able to gain something from these incredible photos. I hope my observations and words help you see a little more than you might have otherwise in Hogan's unparalleled swing.

Beyond the hero of this book and those great players and teachers who shared their ideas about Ben Hogan and/or directly taught me (all of whom are listed in the bibliography), there are other people who have caught my attention with their writings, their impressions of Hogan, their own golf swings, or their teaching concepts related to Hogan. I may or may not have agreed with what they expressed, but at the very least they made me think more about Hogan's swing, and his greatness. These people include Byron Nelson; Gene Borek; Carl Lohren; Chris Toulson; John Mills; Tom Kite; Matt McLean; John C. McLean; Ben Doyle; Andy Brumer; Homer Kelley; Johnny Miller; Ernie Vossler; Rick Belden; Dick, Craig, Butch, and Billy Harmon; Joe Nichols; Bobby Jones; Percy Boomer;

Bob Toski; Doug Ford; Harvey Penick; Dave Collins; Bob Rosburg; Jack Grout; George Knudsen; Greg Norman; Martin Davis; Jules Alexander; Al Mengert; Dave Marr; Bill Melhorn; Dan Jenkins; Lee Trevino; Bill Collins; Bob Watson; Dave Alvarez; Ben Crenshaw; Lanny Wadkins; John Mahaffey; and Ernie Vossler.

A Personal Ben Hogan
Bibliography

While I'm aware that I'm using the term "bibliography" here in an unconventional way, I'm doing so because the people noted below and, indeed, who have appeared throughout this book represent for me a truly special and unparalleled source of knowledge about Ben Hogan. Their generous sharing of stories, insights, inside-the-ropes opinions, and firsthand experiences has enriched not only my understanding of his swing and his game, but also the golf swing, golf in general, and my teaching of the game in particular. The dates next to their names indicate the years I spent learning from them and being friends with these great teachers and players. I feel lucky to have had access to such a personal and authentic reservoir of source material about Hogan and am grateful to these people for the opportunity to share with you what I learned from them. But mostly I feel privileged to call so many of them my friends.

JIMMY BALLARD
1977–present

I personally attended nine of Jimmy Ballard's Two-Day Golf Schools and took private lessons and observed many others. I watched Jimmy teach numerous Tour players and players of all levels.

Jimmy Ballard is ranked among America's greatest teachers. He is one of the best-known instructors in the world and has had many PGA Tour stars and major's winners (including two-time former U.S. Open winner Curtis Strange and former PGA champion Hal Sutton) on his extensive client list. Jimmy, as already mentioned, first worked on the golf swing with Sammy Byrd, who was a professional baseball player turned golf pro, and who eventually won the PGA Championship. (Byrd was actually Babe Ruth's roommate for a time while playing for the New York Yankees.) It was from his work and time spent with Byrd that Ballard developed his concepts of a perfect "connection" in the golf swing for which he and his teaching are known.

At every golf school opening and usually somewhere in his private lessons, Ballard pulled out great pictures of Ben Hogan. Without a doubt Hogan was a key model that Ballard used to build his instructional curriculum at his golf schools. Ballard taught a strict method that knocked teaching in America off its chair, and his analysis of Hogan was very different from the old clichés taught up until he entered the scene. Those clichés included a straight left arm, a full-body turn, keeping the head stationary throughout the swing, driving the knees forward in the through-swing, and finishing in a "reverse C" position, with an arched back. Ballard was ridiculed by the PGA of America, but hundreds of tour players flocked to see him, with great individual success, and today most teachers not only accept his ideas about connection, but treat them as though they had indeed been a teaching staple forever. Amazing!

Ballard taught for the Swedish Golf Federation, which produced Annika Sorenstam, among many other fine players. Sorenstam's swing exemplified everything Ballard taught, though she may not have even known it. Annika dominated women's golf, and no one has ever hit the golf ball straighter and more consistently in the history of the game. In fact, if one were asked to name a player whose game and ball striking most resembled Hogan's, one couldn't go wrong by saying Sorenstam. I went through Ballard's school nine times, paying every time. I also I went down with PGA Tour player Jim Simons every week for private lessons with Ballard. Anyone who does not realize that Ballard was a major figure in the growth of golf schools in America and has contributed tremendously to today's golf instruction ideas and methods does not know golf history. It was a two- to three-month wait to get into a Jimmy Ballard Golf School back then, as Ballard took only fifteen students at a time.

TOMMY BOLT
1981–1984 and sporadically afterward

I had numerous conversations and lessons with Tommy Bolt.

Bolt won the 1958 U.S. Open, tied for third in the Masters in 1952, and had three third-place finishes in the PGA Championship. He won fifteen times on the PGA Tour and three times on the Senior Tour and was inducted into the World Golf Hall of Fame in 2002. He is well known for his temper out on the golf course, though unfortunately not as much for the great ball striker he really was. Bolt played on two Ryder Cup teams in the 1950s.

Bolt told me he copied Hogan's grip as closely as he could, and that he also copied Hogan's ball trajectory, the way Hogan's shots all dropped off slightly in his legendary fade to the right. "Once I saw how Hogan held the club and eliminated the left side of the golf course I was determined to do the same," were Bolt's exact words to me. Bolt was famous for the "no hands" appearance to his release, again something he got directly from observing Hogan.

KEEGAN BRADLEY
2009–present

I worked with Keegan Bradley on many of the things I learned directly from Ken Venturi, which were absolutely Ben Hogan concepts.

When I started working with Bradley he was playing mini tour events and was nearly broke. He won a Hooters Tour event in the first year we worked together and then qualified for the Nationwide tour. In 2011 he qualified for the PGA tour. The rest is history. We continue to work on the things illustrated in this book.

In 2011 Bradley was awarded Rookie of the Year on the PGA Tour and won the PGA Championship.

JOHNNY BULLA
1973–1977

I took lessons with Johnny Bulla and had many conversations with him and played golf with him.

Johnny Bulla played on the PGA Tour, with one win and three runner-up finishes in the majors. He lost the British Open one year on the last hole to a birdie finish by the winner, Richard Burton. All in all, Bulla may be best remembered as a golfer for his seven near misses in major championships. He is also is a member of Carolinas Golf Hall of Fame.

I knew of Bulla before I met him at Papago Park Municipal Golf Course in Phoenix. However, after I spent many days on the range with him I learned a hundred times more, both about him and the game of golf. For example, he was a pilot and often flew Sam Snead and Hogan to tour events. I always made Bulla turn over his club to watch him swing left-handed. You see, Bulla played the tour right-handed, but he was almost as good left-handed, easily shooting under par. In fact, let me take this opportunity to dedicate chapter 7 of this book, with Hogan's image flipped to appear as a left-handed swing sequence, to Bulla. He was a great person and an unbelievable talent.

Bulla was older than Hogan and played with all of the greats of his era, including Bobby Jones, Walter Hagen, Harry Cooper, and Henry Picard. So Bulla really had the experience of watching Hogan progress from a struggling player to the greatest player and ball striker on the planet. When Bulla told me stories of Hogan's work ethic and his progression as a player, I knew I was listening to someone who was really there to see it and understand it firsthand. Johnny confirmed for me that Harry Cooper had helped Hogan, that Hogan was mostly influenced by the swings of Bobby Jones and Jimmy Demaret, and that Hogan was constantly adjusting and working on improving his game.

JACKIE BURKE JR.
1969–present

Jackie Burke is my friend, a mentor, and a teacher.

Jack Burke Jr. was a consistent winner on the PGA Tour in the 1950s, with sixteen wins. He won the 1956 Masters and PGA Championship. He also had a tie for tenth in the U.S.

Open in 1955. Jackie won the Vardon Trophy in 1952 and was voted Player of the Year in 1956. In the Ryder Cup he played on five teams, served as captain twice, and was a special assistant in 2004 for Hal Sutton. A World Golf Hall of Fame member since 2000, he was also given the PGA Tour Lifetime Achievement Award in 2003 and the Bobby Jones Award in 2004. Jackie worked extensively with Jack Nicklaus, Ben Crenshaw, and Phil Mickelson on their putting. All credit Jackie. Along with Jimmy Demaret, Jackie founded Champions Golf Club in Houston.

Jackie Burke's father, Jack Sr., was a great player himself and the finest teacher in America during his era. Young Jackie was taught by his father, who knew Jones and Hogan well. I learned through Jackie Jr. that Hogan used a tremendous amount of Jones's writings, working them into everything he did in his swing. If you look at the writings of Jack Burke Sr. you can see the influence he also had on Hogan. This is not surprising, as Jack Sr. was unbelievably influential for all Texas golf teachers; it was he who taught all of the future Texas instructors his ideas on releasing the golf club with the "no hands" feel, the same exact method Hogan both used himself and instructed his readers to use in his books.

Jackie grew up in a household where all of the great players of that time congregated regularly. From his father he learned the basics of great golf. The first was his grip, which is also the first thing Hogan writes about in *Five Lessons*. (It's worth noting again, as I mention it often in this book, that if you study Jimmy Demaret's grip you will see the grip that would become Hogan's.) Jackie and Hogan were the best of friends and played together all through Hogan's earlier years on the PGA Tour. Jackie was a born teacher, and even as the leading money winner on the PGA Tour he would continue his practice of giving every tour pro a lesson as he went up and down the range at each tournament. Nobody in golf has been more observant than Jackie. Only Demaret knew Hogan better. Those three tough Fort Worth kids formed a link that kept them very close through every year of their lives.

That Jackie Burke was Jack Burke's son did much to help him establish a friendship early on with Hogan. But there was another reason as well. Jackie spent four years in the U.S. Marines, just as Hogan served in the army for two and a half years. Both men were soldiers in World War II, and this did much to cement a bond between them, which while of course centering on golf also transcended it as well, in a manner only veterans of the same war will ever understand.

Jackie would eventually became a main mentor in my life. Can you imagine the number of stories and details I learned about Hogan from him? Jackie told me how Hogan practiced at Champions on his yearly visits there, and how much he respected Demaret, Jackie's co-owner at Champions. It's because of Jackie that I was able to go watch Hogan practice and play at Champions when almost nobody was allowed to observe him at work there. Jackie would also describe how Hogan dissected a golf course and how he intimidated the competition. I was fascinated by all of the details Jackie told me about Hogan's preparation and the rounds those two played together. I learned firsthand from Jackie that Hogan copied Demaret's grip and his ball flight. These kinds of details about Hogan's game and the influences on it could only have come from the people who knew Hogan well.

HARRY COOPER
1975–1992

I taught with Harry Cooper at Westchester Country Club for three years. I took lessons from him, observed him teaching, and had numerous conversations with him.

Cooper, the son of a teaching professional, was born in England but moved to Dallas when he was a child. He won thirty-one times on the PGA Tour in the 1920s and 1930s, but was never able to win a major although he finished well up in the standings in many of them. He finished second in the U.S. Open two times and had ten other top ten finishes in the majors, including second in the 1936 and 1938 Masters. Cooper is still known by many today as the best player never to win a major. He did win the Vardon Trophy in 1937 when he won eight PGA Tour tournaments and was the tour's leading money winner.

I played golf with Cooper. Both of us taught at the club under Bob Watson, a Harvey Penick protégé. Claude Harmon was an assistant pro for Cooper in Chicago, so you can see that there was no shortage of opportunities for these great teachers to share with each other their thoughts about the game and their ideas about how to teach it better. No wonder Harmon credited Cooper for much of what he taught and how he played. Through the years Cooper and I remained good friends, and he helped me tremendously in countless ways. I hope you can see the lineage.

JIMMY DEMARET
1968–1972

I had numerous conversations with Jimmy Demaret at Champions Golf Club and observed him playing and practicing. He is likely the most underrated player in the history of the game.

Demaret won on the PGA Tour thirty-one times throughout his tournament career, which spanned the 1930s, 1940s, and 1950s. Demaret won the Masters three times and had six top tens in the other majors, with a second-place finish in the 1948 U.S. Open. He won the Vardon Trophy in 1947 and was the leading money winner on tour that year. He was inducted into the World Golf Hall of Fame in 1983. Demaret played on three Ryder Cup teams. As mentioned previously and in other places in this book, many who knew Ben Hogan well say that his important grip change at a crucial time in his career, as well as his hand and wrist action that he would use so effectively in his swing as his victories mounted up, were strongly influenced by Demaret's grip and wrist action. Luckily I was able to watch Demaret practice and play golf at various courses in the Houston area. What a talent.

GARDNER DICKINSON
1978–1988

I took lessons from Gardner Dickinson and played many rounds with him at Frenchman's Creek in Florida (a course he designed). I watched him work with numerous Tour players, including Jack Nicklaus, and had many conversations with him on Ben Hogan.

Dickinson won seven times on the PGA Tour in the 1950s, with ten overall professional wins. He was a student and friend of Hogan's and was his teaching assistant at Tamarisk in the early 1950s. Gardner had three top ten finishes in majors, including a tie for sixth in the 1967 U.S. Open and a tie for fifth in the 1965 PGA Championship. He played in seven Masters. His Ryder Cup record from 1967 and 1971 is superb at 9–1–0. Many people agree that Dickinson was more successful in developing a golf swing that resembled Ben Hogan's than many others over the years who attempted to emulate him. Dickinson was one of the many tour pros of that era who also dressed like Hogan on the golf course. Hogan was called the Hawk and Dickinson was referred to as the Chicken Hawk by many of his fellow tour players. He looked like a smaller version of the intense and combative

Hogan. Dickinson was tough as nails but a joy to work with and learn so many Hogan gems.

BEN DOYLE AND HOMER KELLEY
1977–present

I had many conversations with Ben Doyle and took lessons from him and observed him teaching. I spent an entire day at Homer Kelley's house in Seattle, Washington.

Doyle is listed as one of America's 50 Greatest Teachers in *Golf Digest* and in *Golf* magazine's Top 100 Teachers in America and is a lifetime member of the PGA of America.

I knew Doyle well. We played in golf tournaments together around the Northwest. We were both living in Seattle, which was the home of Homer Kelley, the author of *The Golfing Machine*, the in-depth study of the golf swing that has spawned an international group of authorized instructors of the Golfing Machine, of which Doyle was the first.

I took lessons from Doyle when he moved to Carmel Valley Ranch in the Monterey Peninsula area of Northern California. I even used to practice with a young Bobby Clampett, a student of Doyle's from when Clampett was just a little boy. I watched Doyle give a ton of lessons to many golfers of all calibers, and we have stayed in touch to this day. Recently Doyle came to teach at my golf center in Fort Worth. He did a great deal to bring *The Golfing Machine* to the attention of the golf world, and everyone who knows anything about that book and its teachers owes him a great deal.

I went to visit Kelley at his home in Seattle because I wanted to hear his ideas directly from him. When I arrived, I signed in with his wife, Sally, in his guestbook. Then I went with Kelley out to his garage, which was full of plastic plane boards, farming tools, and training aids. His golf bag was there, filled with old golf irons and beat-up woods. It was a strange collection of clubs in a tattered old bag. But he spent that whole day with me going over snap loading, wrist hinge, impact alignments, and other ideas, which he developed and elaborated on in his landmark book.

Kelley had studied Ben Hogan and Sam Snead and saw some differences between the swings of these two greats, and many say that he developed his ideas in *The Golfing Machine* largely from his observations of Hogan's and Snead's swings. Kelley's ideas on Hogan were very mechanical and seemed to me to have been strongly influenced by his reading of Hogan's books. I wonder if he ever saw Hogan or Snead hit a shot. His own swing was not impressive, but Kelley was a researcher and writer and not a tournament player. Ben Doyle was the first teaching pro to bring his detailed writings to the world. Kelley's ideas and his book's influence then began to spread widely, making their way to, among others, Tom Tomasello, Gregg McHatton, and Lynn Blake (these three, along with Doyle, were among the select group of the first instructors of the Golfing Machine to have been authorized by Kelley himself). The book also greatly influenced the thoughts and teaching of Mac O'Grady and Jim Hardy (perhaps best known today as the teacher of the One Plane/Two Plane swing theory). The influence of *The Golfing Machine* is very much alive today, with Andy Plummer and Mike Bennett, "creators" of the Stack and Tilt method, and even Sean Foley, Tiger Woods's present coach, all crediting the book (the ideas all brought to the golf world by Ben Doyle) as a major influence in the development of their teaching and swing philosophies and methods.

The point I'm making here is that much of today's golf swing schools/theories/methods—call them what you will—have very strong roots in Hogan's swing. I think it's fair to say that as long as intelligent and talented teachers, researchers, and writers continue to publish golf instruction, in books and other media, Hogan will remain a central and important source of that material.

JACK FLECK
2007–2009

I played golf and had many conversations with Jack Fleck, and I read his accounts of the 1955 U.S. Open.

Fleck's Ben Hogan story has endured as one of the most fascinating and colorful among all that have combined to create (to quote a very good book's title) the "Hogan Mystique." Fleck was a little-known driving-range pro from Iowa who had little success playing the tour before he managed to beat Hogan in an eighteen-hole playoff to win the 1955 U.S. Open at the Olympic Club in San Francisco. Most golf historians agree that Fleck's Open victory over Hogan was the greatest upset in the history of the game, and some sports writers have even called it the greatest upset in the history of all sports.

Years later I met Fleck and played a little golf with him. He loved Hogan's swing, and after visualizing many of his moves worked them into his own swing. It was great to watch Fleck demonstrate these moves to me in full detail. Notice I said "demonstrate," because he struggled to verbalize the "feel" of his own golf swing. This is not uncommon among many good or great players, and in fact many of them find it impossible to put the technical and feel aspects of their swing into words. Notice as well that I emphasize their *own* swing, because a lot of the great players of Hogan's era, including some of the ones you've read about in this book, went on to become marvelous teachers of the game.

Actually, Hogan in his two books, *Power Golf* and *Five Lessons*, communicates what he knows *and feels* about swinging a golf club and playing the game with unparalleled clarity, intelligence, and style. It's just one of the very many ways

Hogan stood head and shoulders above his peers. In fact, I can make the argument that *Five Lessons* stands as the most influential golf instruction book ever written. Tell me another book that has influenced more tour players and top teachers over the years. Anyone? But back to Fleck.

Al Mengert really gave me the insider's story of Fleck's upset Open win over Hogan. In fact, Mengert, Walker Inman, and Mike Krak were all good friends who had qualified for that Open and who played a Wednesday practice round that week with Fleck. According to Mengert, Fleck played as bad a round that day as he had ever seen by a good player. So you can imagine Mengert's surprise when after finishing his play round on Sunday's final round and while sipping a beer in the locker room, he saw Fleck's charge on television that included his birdying two of the last four holes. Fleck's heroics tied Hogan and forced the playoff he won the next day. (As an aside, this was the very first golf tournament ever broadcast on live TV.)

"Are there two Jack Flecks?" Mengert asked the bartender in the clubhouse while watching incredulously as Fleck's finish unfolded—the struggling player he had witnessed on Wednesday, and now this one about to catch and tie the greatest golfer of his time. It was the same guy!

Interestingly, Fleck was the only player other than Hogan himself to use Hogan Company clubs that week. Also, like Ken Venturi and Gardner Dickinson, Fleck wore the Hogan cap. Even more incredible is that before play began on Thursday, Hogan personally delivered to Fleck two special wedges from the Hogan club factory, ground specifically for Fleck's game and the Open's course conditions at the Olympic Club. Amazing.

Fleck told me that he had prepared himself for Hogan not to say a word to him during the playoff, but in fact Hogan was nice to him all day. He added that Hogan was very gracious in defeat as well, dispelling another myth about Hogan that he never expressed feelings out on the golf course.

CLAUDE HARMON AND MY "WINGED FOOT CIRCLE"
1975–present

I saw Claude Harmon for lessons beginning in 1975 at Winged Foot and later at Morningside. I had weekly lunches with him in Rancho Mirage, California.

Claude Harmon won the 1948 Masters as a club pro. He finished third in the 1959 U.S. Open. Harmon's great teaching career, which began after he finished competing on the tour, included head professional positions at Winged Foot Country Club, Seminole Golf Club, and Thunderbird Country Club.

After I stopped playing professional golf full-time (I missed qualifying at the final stage of tour school in 1977), I went back to Houston to see the man who would be one of my main mentors: Jackie Burke. I had been offered a great opportunity in real estate by a Houston businessman but was unsure about what I wanted to do. Burke put me in touch with three top private clubs in New York and told me the Metropolitan Section of the PGA of America was the only place to go to work in the golf business. He said I would teach a lot there and would have the winters off to continue playing professional golf events if that's what I wanted to do. I drove back to interview with Harmon at Thunderbird in Rancho Mirage, California, which was Harmon's winter job (he worked as the head pro at Winged Foot during the spring and summer). Ultimately I was hired by Wes Ellis (another great tour player) at the famed Westchester Country Club in Rye, New York. Although I would have loved a job at Winged Foot, the choice I made allowed me to run a junior program with over a hundred kids and teach players at all levels. I also taught with five other top teachers including Harry Cooper, Mary Lena Faulk (twenty-six LPGA Tour wins and a Penick protégée), and Mary Bryant, who still does TV work for NBC. Westchester Country Club is very close to Winged Foot, and I went over there often. One of my great friends, Lee Alexander (who played at Wake Forest when I played at Houston), was one of the assistants. Another assistant was Kelley Moser, who would later be my partner in the Metropolitan pro-pro event, which we won twice. I got to know Harmon much better there and learned so much about teaching and Ben Hogan from him.

FREDDIE HAWKINS
1976–1980

I played golf with Freddie Hawkins and took lessons from him. We talked many times about Ben Hogan, and he helped me understand how Hogan putted.

Hawkins played on the PGA Tour from the mid-1940s to the mid-1960s. He won a Tour event in Oklahoma, and played on the 1957 Ryder Cup team for captain Jackie Burke Jr. Hawkins placed second nineteen times on the PGA Tour. He tied for second in the 1958 Masters and tied for sixth in the 1957 Masters.

I played numerous times with Hawkins, who was the original "Hawk" until Hogan took over that moniker. Hawkins played many times with Hogan and provided me with some great insights. He was sure Hogan was at his best, as Hogan himself has said, in 1948 and 1949, before his devastating car accident.

BOBBY JONES
1974–present

I read all of the books and pamphlets from Bobby Jones and compared them to the writings of Hogan. I played golf with Jones's son at Augusta.

Jones was inducted into the World Golf Hall of Fame in 1974. He was the founder and co-designer of Augusta National Golf Club and the Masters Tournament in 1934, and is always prominent in any discussion about who is the greatest golfer of all time. In 1930 he culminated his championship career in golf by winning in the same year the four major championships of that era, the U.S. Amateur, the British Amateur, the U.S. Open, and the Open Championship. The accomplishment was known then as the Grand Slam, and though the Masters and the PGA Championship have replaced the U.S. Amateur and the British Amateur to comprise today's four majors, nobody has won the Grand Slam since. Jones is the winner of four U.S. Opens, three Open Championships, five U.S. Amateurs, and one British Amateur. He is the author of *Down the Fairway*, *Golf Is My Game*, *Bobby Jones on Golf*, and *Bobby Jones on the Basic Golf Swing*.

I've studied Jones's writings and feel very comfortable in saying that Ben Hogan in his own two books used many of the same descriptions and phrases written previously by Jones. I know Hogan admired everything about Jones, including his intellect and his advice on the golf swing.

JOHN MAHAFFEY
1968–present

John Mahaffey was my roommate at the University of Houston. I observed him playing with Ben Hogan, and I had numerous conversations with him on Hogan.

Mahaffey won ten times on the PGA Tour and has one Champions Tour victory to date. He had four top tens in majors, including his win in the 1978 PGA Championship at Oakmont Country Club and a second-place finish in the 1975 U.S. Open. Mahaffey played on the 1979 Ryder Cup team. He also finished runner-up to Jerry Pate when Pate hit the miracle

5-iron over the lake in Atlanta to one inch for a tap-in birdie to win the U.S. Open.

At the University of Houston, Mahaffey and I shared a room for one year and played a lot of golf, and he went on to have a great career on the PGA Tour. Since Mahaffey was built like Hogan, was a Texas boy like Hogan, and played using Hogan equipment, he got to spend precious time with Hogan, both taking lessons and playing golf with him. He was one of just a few young players Hogan took an interest in helping. I owe and offer Mahaffey my thanks for sharing with me some of the "real stuff" stories about and insights into Hogan. It was also great to see my roommate actually play with the man. Priceless.

AL MENGERT
1965–1980

I took lessons from Al Mengert and caddied for him in tournaments and played numerous rounds of golf with him.

Mengert was a champion amateur in the Pacific Northwest before turning to the professional tour. He played on the PGA Tour for twenty years. Mengert was the director of golf for fourteen years at the historic Oakland Hills Country Club near Detroit, but his connection to Ben Hogan came as a result of his having worked under Claude Harmon, who was extremely close to Hogan. From Harmon, Hogan learned much on the lateral motion in the golf swing. Mengert spoke often of the importance of good legwork in the swing and of how Hogan's swing reflected the excellent use of his legs that he learned from Harmon. He was the head pro at Tacoma Country Club in Washington State before moving to Oakland Hill, and as a Washington State native myself, I had the great fortune to work with him from age fifteen to nineteen. Like anyone who ever saw Hogan play, Mengert was in awe of him. "My swing looks like the mechanical man, while Hogan looks like Fred Astaire,"

Mengert said to me, even though he had one of the most beautiful swings anyone could imagine—except when compared with Hogan's! I played the best golf of my life working with Mengert. Too bad he left the northwest.

JOHNNY MILLER
1972–present

I had many conversations about Ben Hogan with Johnny Miller and the impact Hogan had on his game. Hogan did a clinic with Miller in Mexico and visited him at his home in Silverado, California.

Miller made the most incredible remark about Hogan (on videotape): "Ben Hogan is the only golfer in the history of the game who actually said he had figured out the swing. No great player has said they had it, but Hogan did." I use to trade golf clubs with a young Miller up at his Silverado home. Later I played with him in professional events and did a clinic with him. We have remained friends through the years. I think most golf viewers realize that Miller is the foremost expert on the details of the golf swing, well ahead of all the broadcast analysts. I played with him during the time he dominated golf. His ball striking for a period of time rivaled the greatest in history. That's why I put a large value on what Miller says about Hogan. Even though Miller is a player and not a true teacher or serious swing researcher, he has the intuitive skills of a great instructor. He has world-class insight. I always greatly enjoy the time I get to speak with him, the clinic we did together in Mexico, as well as his commentary on TV.

MOE NORMAN
1974–2000

I played many tournaments paired with Moe Norman, a Canadian legend, on the Canadian Tour and the winter Florida

Tour during the years I competed, from 1974 to 1980. Mo talked extensively about Ben Hogan with me and the influence that Hogan had on his swing. Norman was a great player and won more than forty Canadian PGA Tour events. He delighted the galleries with his shot-making expertise. Until his death, he would do a clinic or perform at the Canadian Open event that was attended by many current U.S. PGA Tour stars. He was amazing.

The great thing about watching Norman practice was his control of the golf ball on all of the shots. He was not afraid to talk about how he did it. I certainly listened intently. Norman would talk to anyone, comparing his swing to Hogan's, for as long as the person chose to listen. The practice sessions and rounds of golf both casual and competitive with Norman provided me with valuable insight into the technique of both Hogan and Norman.

TONEY PENNA AND JACK GROUT
1976–1978

I had numerous lessons and conversations with Toney Penna at Frenchman's Creek in Florida. He played in the Ben Hogan era and built clubs for Hogan when Hogan played MacGregor equipment. I took lessons from Jack Grout and observed him teaching and had conversations with him about Hogan and Jack Nicklaus.

Penna built the Ben Hogan model drivers for MacGregor, as well as Hogan's own drivers that he used in play. Penna told me that Ben's personal drivers were very flat-faced, didn't have much loft, and had very open clubfaces to accommodate his legendary power fade. He said the grips were extra large and were set with the reminder very open as well, meaning that Hogan positioned the straight ridge of what's called a "reminder grip" to the left of the grip's center line. Of course, I know all of this is true, because, as I've written, I picked up all of Hogan's clubs myself and studied his driver. I met Penna in 1976 at Frenchman's Creek in Palm Beach Gardens, Florida, when I was working with Gardner Dickinson there. The three of us had numerous lunches together, and the conversation would often turn to Hogan. I also did an interview with Penna. He was a good pro player, and truly one of the greatest club designers of all time. He said Hogan knew everything about golf clubs, as Hogan worked on clubs and built them himself when he was a youngster at Glen Garden Country Club in Fort Worth. I never played golf with Penna, but we talked about the swing a lot. He was very old at that time, and though he still did hit balls on the range, he no longer played.

Jack Grout, Jack Nicklaus's first teacher (other than his father), worked with Nicklaus during this same time period on the same range at Frenchman's Creek. I spoke with Grout there often, and took lessons from him too, and both watched Nicklaus and Grout on the practice tee many times and then discussed with him the lessons he gave the Golden Bear. We also sometimes spoke about Jackie Burke, whom Grout loved. Grout greatly admired Hogan and said he had the most control of the golf ball of any player he ever saw. That's quite a statement from the teacher of the player many consider the greatest of all time, Jack Nicklaus. So there at Frenchman's Creek Country Club you had Gardner Dickinson, Jack Grout, and Toney Penna all at the same time. What a place!

JOHNNY REVOLTA
1976–1988

I watched Johnny Revolta teach and took lessons from him, and I sent students to him. I spoke with Revolta on his work with Ben Hogan, Claude Harmon, and Ken Venturi.

Revolta played on the PGA Tour from the mid-1930s to the mid-1950s, winning eighteen times. He won five times in

1935, including the PGA Championship. Revolta also played on the Ryder Cup teams in 1935 and 1937. He was a master of the short game, and his book *Johnny Revolta's Short Cuts to Better Golf* is still in print.

Of all the many great teachers I have personally worked with and watched, it would be hard for me to place any of them above Revolta. I took many lessons from him and sent many of my students to him. I couldn't wait to hear what they thought of that experience. All of them loved their lessons. Revolta had an incredible history of working with players at every level; he taught everyone from beginners to Hall of Famers. He once taught at Tamarisk Country Club, where I was the director of golf, Hogan was the head professional, and Angel de la Torre and even the excellent tour player Gardner Dickinson (who modeled his swing, game, and even style of dress on Hogan's) taught after they finished playing. I wonder if any other club has ever had a group of teachers of this caliber. When I served at Tamarisk I saw the results of their work. Most of the old-time members there had wonderful technique, and all chipped and pitched the ball nicely. I know Claude Harmon learned a ton from Revolta, as Claude also taught in the Palm Springs area, at Thunderbird, for twenty years. Harmon was rightfully considered the greatest bunker player and bunker teacher in the history of golf, but I watched Revolta teach in an almost identical style. (Revolta played the tour about twenty years prior to Harmon.) Revolta taught Harmon a ton about the short game and how to hold off bunker shots and pitch shots. He too witnessed the development of Hogan firsthand, and among other insights he shared with me was that he felt Hogan learned his wrist action from the great players who went before him, especially Jimmy Demaret.

I first watched Revolta teach when I played the mini tours in Southern California. My roommate then worked full-time with Revolta, and I drove over with him to the club numerous times to watch Revolta teach. When I was working at Tamarisk I'd often make the relatively short drive over to Mission Hills, where Revolta finished his teaching career and where they named the driving range after him. Speaking with him about Hogan was like being there myself watching Hogan play and practice. Revolta was a vivid orator and an extremely direct person. In short, there is an unmistakable instruction lineage of the teaching of the "modern," or even the contemporary, golf swing that began with Revolta and Jackie Burke Sr., then was continued by Harry Cooper and Jack Grout (the young Jack Nicklaus's golf teacher), who passed it on to Harmon, Ken Venturi, Jackie Burke Jr., and Dickinson. I've done my best to learn all I could from these great teachers and men and continue to strive to carry on in my teaching and writing and my DVD, Internet, and TV work this marvelous and hallowed tradition.

DOUG SANDERS
1990–present

Doug Sanders is a friend of mine. I took lessons with Sanders as well as gave him lessons. I studied his ideas on the golf swing and the impact Ben Hogan had on his swing.

Sanders had twenty PGA Tour wins, two other professional wins, and one Senior Tour win. He achieved thirteen top tens in the major championships and finished second in the 1966 and 1970 Open Championship, second in the 1959 PGA Championship, and second in the 1958 U.S. Open. Sanders learned a great deal from Ben Hogan both via personal observation and through his lessons with Johnny Revolta. Though Sanders is known for his very short swing, Sanders's flat downswing shaft plane very much resembles Hogan's, as does his long-right-arm follow-through. Unfortunately, he is also known to many for the 30-inch putt he missed to win the 1970 British Open, a tournament he would finish second in to Jack Nicklaus after an eighteen-hole playoff. Doug has his flaws, but he has been great to me, and was a major source of information on Hogan. Without any doubt, Sanders was one of the really great ball strikers.

GENE SARAZEN
1977–1980

I played numerous 18-hole rounds of golf with Gene Sarazen. I took lessons from him and spoke to him in detail about Ben Hogan.

Sarazen was a star player in the 1920s, winning the 1922 U.S. Open and PGA Championship. He won thirty-nine PGA tournaments and was a member of the Ryder Cup team six times in the 1920s and 1930s. Sarazen and Ben Hogan are two of five men to have won the modern Grand Slam, which consists of the Masters (won once by Sarazen), the U.S. Open (two wins), the British Open (one win), and the PGA Championship (three wins). The other three modern Slam winners are Jack Nicklaus, Tiger Woods, and Gary Player. Sarazen was inducted into the World Golf Hall of Fame in 1974. Other awards of his include the PGA Tour Lifetime Achievement Award, the Bobby Jones Award, and the AP Male Athlete of the Year in 1932. Also, Sarazen is credited with inventing the modern sand wedge that he used to win the Open Championship in 1932. Though I didn't know Sarazen well, the time I spent with him and the rounds of golf I played with him proved incredibly meaningful to me both in terms of the thoughts he shared with me on Hogan and about the golf swing and playing the game itself. Those hours with Sarazen remain among the greatest highlights of my life.

SAM SNEAD
1995–1998

I played golf with Sam Snead and went to the Masters and stayed in the same home with him twice. Snead and I did a DVD together and spoke extensively about Ben Hogan. We also made several appearances together on the Golf Channel.

Snead, known as Slammin' Sammy, or just sometimes "the Slammer," had an unsurpassed career, which included 165 professional wins worldwide, eighty-two of them on the PGA Tour (still the record for the most wins ever), and fourteen wins on the Senior Tour. Snead won seven majors, including three Masters, three PGA Championships, and one British Open (with four second-place finishes in that event). He finished second in the U.S. Open four times, and the fact that he never captured his nation's championship, the U.S. Open, represented one of the very few disappointments that he has spoken of in an otherwise charmed life in golf. Snead is a Golf Hall of Fame member and received the PGA Tour Lifetime Achievement Award in 1998. He was the leading money winner on tour three times and was a Vardon Trophy winner four times.

I was fortunate to spend a good deal of time with the legendary Snead. He was, of course, a contemporary of Hogan's and always his fierce competitor, but maybe even more so between 1946 and 1948. Snead and I did a comprehensive VHS video together on Snead and his swing in 1999. I spent three days at the Homestead in West Virginia with him and also did two special Golf Channel shows with and about him. On one of my trips to the Masters I stayed in a rented home with Snead. From our many conversations I learned that he had a deep respect for Hogan, so one can chalk up the idea that the two men did not like one another as another false Hogan myth. However, mixed in with the great things he told me about Hogan was one thing that always bothered him. In 1950 Snead won ten PGA Tour events while Hogan won only one, the U.S. Open. Even so, Hogan won Player of the Year from the PGA of America that year, and Snead was stunned when that happened. Snead and Ken Venturi were two of the pallbearers at Hogan's funeral. "That's how Ben would have wanted it," said Hogan's wife, Valerie.

Snead was also one of golf's great raconteurs. While he was, as I've said, respectful toward Hogan, the two men were unquestionably rivals, as the tone of the following story reveals. Speaking about Hogan's legendary accuracy, someone told Snead that "when Hogan played thirty-six holes on the same course in a day, he would hit his drives on the second eighteen into the divot holes of his iron shots from his first round," to which Snead quickly quipped, "If he was so accurate, why didn't he *miss* the divots?"

PETER THOMPSON
1990–1991

I observed Peter Thompson playing at Sleepy Hollow in the Senior Tour event. I spoke to him in detail about Ben Hogan's influence on his own golf swing.

Thompson was a winner of five British Opens (three in a row). He won eighty-one professional events, six of them on the PGA Tour and eleven on the Senior Tour. He won twenty-six times on the European Tour. Thompson tied for fifth in the 1957 Masters and fourth in the 1956 U.S. Open. He is a member of the World Golf Hall of Fame and received the Arnold Palmer Award in 1986. Thompson is a renowned golf writer and was the club professional at the Royal Melbourne Golf Club in Australia, designed by Alister MacKenzie and one of the world's greatest golf courses. Thompson has also done a lot of work as a television golf analyst.

I met Thompson when he played at Sleepy Hollow Country Club in the Golf Digest Commemorative Senior Tour event. I spent a lot of time with him that week. Previously I had played eighteen holes with him at PGA West. As usual, I loved talking to great players about their golf swing and ideas on the game. Thompson loved Ben Hogan and told me he modeled his swing after Hogan's. Though it may sound curious, this was the main reason he never watched his own swing on TV or in videos. Even though I would videotape him hitting balls, he would not look at the film. Thompson said he visualized the Hogan moves, and while he was sure he had the feel for the Hogan swing, he was equally sure that, as he said, "My swing would not really look like Hogan's." Therefore, while he often studied films of Hogan's swing, he felt that looking at his own would be counterproductive to his game.

Thompson's perspective speaks to a common modern teaching axiom that "feel isn't always real," and indeed tolls a cautionary bell about it. What the teaching pros who use this expression mean is that the visual evidence of a player's recorded swing may not look like the internal image that player has of his or her own golf swing. Well, Peter had a feel that worked so well for him in his actual swing and game, and he didn't want to confuse himself by seeing that although he tried to copy Hogan's swing, his didn't look like Hogan's at all. Thompson was that rare individual who placed all of his confidence in his feel. For him, the video lied and his "feel was real." Of course, I've reiterated in this book that inaccurate or imprecise filming of a player's swing, as too many teaching pros still do today, can be more harmful than helpful to a player's progress. Perhaps Thompson just had too many experiences with people filming his swing sloppily, but this is a discussion best saved for another day.

Thompson won nine Senior Tour events in one year and then went back to Australia, which has remained his home base ever since. He was a great player and is a very intelligent man. He came down once to my Superstation at Sleepy Hollow and watched some of my Hogan videos, which he really loved doing. We talked about his image of Hogan's swing, which he cultivated in his mind, and what he looked and felt in his own golf swing, and he remained confident in his decision not to have his own swing taped.

LEE TREVINO
1986–present

I had many conversations with Lee Trevino regarding Ben Hogan and the influence Hogan had on his entire golf game.

What an incredible opportunity I had when Lee played in the Senior Tour event at Sleepy Hollow Country Club. I was the director of golf hosting the event. Lee Trevino, as anyone involved in golf knows, was a huge Ben Hogan fan. In fact, he copied Hogan's ball flight. He had to change his setup to accomplish that goal, but he did it and became one of the few players to "own his swing." Trevino provided me with phenomenal swing ideas as I shadowed him constantly in his appearances at SHCC. Watching Trevino hit a golf ball reminded everyone of Hogan. He hit that beautiful controlled fade and could repeat it under any and all conditions. I personally heard Hogan say, "Lee Trevino is no fluke. He will win many majors." This was in 1969, after Trevino's first U.S. Open win and when many so called experts wrote that Trevino was a flash in the pan.

KEN VENTURI
1975–present

Ken Venturi is a great friend of mine. I've had numerous conversations with him and taken many lessons from him over the years. I worked for Venturi at Marco Island, Florida. We've played literally hundreds of rounds together.

Venturi had fourteen PGA Tour wins and one major championship, the 1964 U.S. Open. He finished second twice at the Masters Tournament, once as an amateur, and notched ten top tens in the majors overall. He was a 1965 Ryder Cup team player, a Ryder Cup captain, the 1964 *Sports Illustrated* Sportsman of the Year award winner, and the 1998 Old Tom Morris Award winner from the Golf Course Superintendents Association of America, and he worked in the television booth for thirty-four years as the lead golf analyst for CBS Sports. Venturi taught John Cook, Tom Watson, Tom Weiskopf, George Knudson, and hundreds of other Tour professionals. He's a true living treasure of American golf. His two mentors were considered the best of all time, Byron Nelson and Ben Hogan. Nelson was quoted as saying, "Ken Venturi was the greatest iron player I ever saw."

I met Venturi at Westchester Country Club just north of New York City in 1975. We became good friends after I went out to Palm Springs to work on my game with him over the winter of 1975–1976, and we started playing many rounds together after that winter. We usually played at Bermuda Dunes out in the desert, which at that time was one of the courses in the rotation of the Bob Hope Tour, one of the great celebrity pro-am tournaments, held early each year and that still bears the late great comedian's name. In 1977 Venturi took the director of golf position at Marco Island Country Club in Florida. I finished second at stage one of tour school that fall but missed qualifying for the PGA Tour at Pinehurst in the final stage. After that I worked for Venturi at Marco Island and began to focus more and more of my energy on teaching. It was there that I met Gene Sarazen, who was seventy-eight years old, while I was twenty-four. He and Venturi were great friends, and I got along wonderfully with Sarazen. I played eight or nine rounds with him, always eighteen holes and always for a wager. He played from the white tees, but never shot over 72 in our competition.

My talks with Venturi and Sarazen often drifted into detailed ideas about the golf swing. Sarazen was very bright and knew tons about the swing, and Venturi was the most knowledgeable person I had ever met on advanced shotmaking. He could still do it all when I played with him. It was nothing to see him flag every iron shot for however many holes we played. At Marco Island, Venturi had the fastest cart I've ever been in, now or then. It went 45 miles per hour, and since he hated to wait we almost never played a consecutive eighteen holes. We passed groups while they were standing still. Some never knew we skipped ahead of them! That's the way Venturi was and still is, a fast player and a fast thinker. How else could he have been the lead analyst for CBS golf for over thirty-four consecutive years?

This book is filled with insights about Ben Hogan that I learned from Venturi, and I couldn't have written it without him.

CARL WELTY
1966–present

Carl Welty is a friend of mine as well as a research partner. I've had many lessons with Welty and numerous conversations.

Originally from San Diego, Welty is a PGA member and is ranked as a *Golf* magazine Top 100 Teacher in America. He has worked with me at the Jim McLean Golf School at PGA West in La Quinta, California, since 1997, though he is also available for golf lessons at the Grand in Del Mar, just north of San Diego. Carl worked as a PGA apprentice under the legendary Paul Runyan, a former PGA champion, who also competed in the very first Masters and later went on to become best known as a teacher specializing in the short game. Welty has had an extensive career in golf instruction, with numerous accolades, and has played an invaluable role in the development of golf instruction for the Jim McLean Golf Schools and in many other projects of mine. Welty started the first golf school west of the Mississippi at the La Costa Resort and Spa in 1983, and held the position as director of instruction there for twelve years.

Simply put, Welty taught me how to research golf swings. He is the king of that science, and nobody has come close to the work he has done in the field.

When he first showed me how to dissect a swing on videotape, I was totally impressed with the degree of detail and precision with which he looked at golf swings. This was back in the 1970s when we used reel-to-reel videotape, which represented an advancement from 8mm film, or the sequence camera we used prior to that to shoot swings in still photography. As video improved it clearly became the best tool for studying golf swings, as we could instantly stop the tape and replay any part of it that we wanted. Like a top football coach, Welty would play and replay sections of a golf swing over and over. Right from the beginning we studied Ben Hogan's swing this way, and as video systems improved even more, with video clips easily transferred to computers, I would say we looked at Hogan's swing hundreds of thousands of times. Welty is a maniac on doing a study correctly. Because he knew that looking at a golf swing from a slightly different camera angle from swing to swing changed one's clear observation and the analysis of that swing, he insisted that the camera angle and the distance from the golfer under study match up and be identical each and every time.

If you look at old footage of great players' swings shot down the target line, you quickly discern that the cameraman almost always stood directly behind the golfer and on that target line, as this was the only way the viewer could see the ball flight. If the camera was located inside the target line the ball appeared to go straight to the right as if it were flying off the screen and not down the fairway or practice range. So the best clips we took off TV were shot down the line, as was recommended in a book Welty used (and introduced me to) called *The Search for the Perfect Swing*, published in 1967. That's how we did it back then, and that is how all of my teachers shoot video at my golf schools to this day. It's absolutely true that I could not have written this book had it not been for all I learned from Welty on the very best way to study and analyze golf swings using video.

I also know that our visually recording golf swings in such an accurate manner is the reason I have been chosen to do so much work over the years for the Golf Channel. It's one of the reasons I've been invited to talk about golf to audiences all over the world and have had the opportunity to write and publish books. The knowledge I gained from decades of detailed study with Welty cannot be faked, and together we found many groundbreaking ideas on the swing. Not the least significant of these was our commitment to finding and identifying what the players actually did in their golf swings versus what they said they did. Golfers might say that they have made a big swing change or are doing something new in their swings. From studying film in the precise manner we do, always from the same correct camera angles, we can tell if what they say is true or not.

Our meticulous checking of Hogan's swing, and the changes he made to it in the manner detailed above, is one reason, I can proudly say, I've won major awards for the videos I've produced on Hogan. It couldn't have happened without Welty. In fact, my belief in the method we use in studying golfers' swings has given me the confidence I needed to continue to study Hogan's swing over so many years.

The lesson to be learned here? You have to do golf swing research *precisely and carefully*! You have to throw out bad clips. You cannot compare Hogan's swings or anyone else's shot from different camera angles, because then you will not have a solid base and basis from which to make accurate comparisons and draw truthful, verifiable conclusions. Almost all golf teachers base their research on the golf swing by using video shot from different and often wildly erratic angles. Therefore their "conclusions" amount to nothing more than their opinions. It doesn't pass the rudimentary rules of scientific research. It's pretend research at best and is worthless to me.

Welty proved to me that Hogan in the late 1940s was at his best and that the swing after the accident was virtually identical, except for his slight loss of power and the intense time it took him to prepare himself each day to play a round of golf. The swing was there, but the body was not. Hogan could never play a full schedule after the 1949 accident, but he sure could still hit a golf ball better than any man alive.

Further Resources

The Hogan Way, by John Andrisani (New York: HarperCollins, 2000)

Andrisani provides the reader with some guidance through the history and development of Hogan's swing and highlights specific recommendations. The book provides no serious documentation on how the swing was developed. Through drawings and photos from 1966, the author asserts that Hogan's swing evolved over time. There are various quotes and observations from other instructors that provide supportive perspectives on Hogan's swing elements. The work does not give a definitive description of Hogan's swing from his glory days prior to his accident in 1949. Andrisani helped organize my revolutionary manual on teaching golf, *The Eight-Step Swing,* which was published in 1993.

Ben Hogan: The Man behind the Mystique, by Martin Davis (Greenwich, CT: American Golfer, 2002)

> Newly discovered photos of the incomparable Ben Hogan, with articles by Valerie Hogan with Dave Anderson ("The Ben Hogan I Knew") and Dan Jenkins ("Hogan Lore Strikes Again"), eyewitness accounts by John Derr, and my own swing analysis.

The Hogan Mystique, by Martin Davis (Greenwich, CT: American Golfer, 2004 [1994])

> Classic photographs of the great Ben Hogan by Jules Alexander, with articles by Dave Anderson ("The Standards of the Man"), Ben Crenshaw ("The Hawk"), and Dan Jenkins ("Hogan His Ownself"), and commentary by Ken Venturi. The photos were taken during practice rounds for the 1959 U.S. Open at Winged Foot Country Club in New York.

Ben Hogan: An American Life, by James Dodson (New York: Doubleday, 2004)

> A thorough and thoughtful biography of Ben Hogan that was authorized by the estate of Ben and Valerie Hogan.

Power Golf, by Ben Hogan (Cranbury, NJ: A. S. Barnes, 1948)

> Personally written by Ben Hogan in the late 1940s, this instructional work provides a description of many aspects of golf, similar to many previous instructional works by prominent golfers before him. This is Hogan's own perspective on tournament golf, the basics of the golf swing, golf equipment, and on-course shotmaking. The text is accompanied by a series of still photographs of Hogan's swings taken at Augusta National Golf Club. This is a brilliant book written by Hogan himself with no ghostwriter. You'll find just about everything here, as in the later, more famous *Five Lessons*.

Five Lessons: The Modern Fundamentals of Golf, by Ben Hogan with Herbert Warren Wind and drawings by Anthony Ravielli (Cranbury, NJ: A. S. Barnes, 1957)

> Golf writer Wind and illustrator Ravielli assist Hogan in compiling what Hogan believes are the most important fundamentals of the modern golf swing, so that golfers of average physical ability who via study and practice incorporate these fundamentals into their golf swing will break 80 in a relatively short time. While clearly stating what Hogan considered the fundamentals of the golf swing, the book falls short of describing Hogan's movements, and the drawings are done from static photographs, not in-motion photography. Almost everything in this book can be found in Hogan's first book, *Power Golf.* It is, however, the classic Hogan book and is filled with priceless information.

The Fundamentals of Hogan, by David Leadbetter with Lorne Rubenstein (New York: Sleeping Bear Press / Doubleday, 2000)

> Using numerous original photographs taken in 1955–1956 by Anthony Ravielli as source material for his illustrations in *Five Lessons: The Modern Fundamentals of Golf,* David Leadbetter provides his expert perspective and analysis of the Hogan golf swing and Hogan's "fundamentals." The book provides some new wrinkles and challenges to Hogan's concepts, but I found it hard to discern clear positive points. I respectfully have to disagree with several important conclusions. You can see the differences clearly in this book.

Hogan, by Curt Sampson (Nashville: Rutledge Hill Press, 1996)

> A biography on Ben Hogan that provides wonderful insights to his life, career, and the qualities that created the mystical aura surrounding the golf legend.

DVDs

Ben Hogan: The Golf Swing DVD, by the Golf Channel, with my own analysis, 2004

> Best-selling analysis of Ben Hogan's swing that he used in 1953 to win the Triple Crown of golf: the Masters Tournament, the U.S. Open, and the Open Championship at Carnoustie.

The Ben Hogan Collection DVD set, with *The Swing Revealed* interactive software, by McTee's Champions LLC, Tom McCarthy, executive producer, 2006

> Extensive unique footage of Ben Hogan and his golf swing throughout his career. Clear, concise analysis by me on Hogan's swing fundamentals, including commentary on Hogan's secret and X- and Y-Factor analysis. Special features include "Swing Gallery" and "Career Summary." The PC software has "motion control" capability to view four different angles of Hogan's swing.